The Earth V

The Earth Will Teach You

Kevin Durrant

Published in 2014 by Wide Margin,
90 Sandyleaze, Gloucester, GL2 0PX, UK
http://www.wide-margin.co.uk/

What the Donkey Saw reprinted by permission of Enitharmon; We are making a new world reprinted by permission of the Imperial War Museum; The Moor reprinted by permission of Phoenix; Sighting the Slave Ship reprinted by permission of Bloodaxe; Screened Porch reprinted by permission of Carcanet Press; February - Not Everywhere reprinted by permission of Berlinn.

The Great Awk reprinted by kind permission of The Lost Bird Project; Oil reprinted by kind permission of David Parkins. Cover photograph by kind permission of Caroline Cobb.

All efforts have been made to locate and contact rightsholders of other works appearing in this book, which are reprinted for the purposes of critical commentary.

ISBN 978-1-908860-07-1

Printed and bound in Great Britain by Lightning Source, Milton Keynes

Contents

Preface   vii

Introduction   ix

Part I   Listening to the Voices   1

1   The Beaten Donkey   3

2   The Protective Tree   13

3   The Humble Soil   23

4   The Devious Snake   33

5   The Exhausted Land   45

6   The Mighty Crocodile   53

7   The Sacred Oak   67

8   The Bumper Crop   79

9   The Barren Slopes   91

10 The Mysterious Cloud   101

11 The Restricted Corn   111

Part II   Moving to the Rhythm   125

12 The Rising Sun   127

13 The Lengthening Shadows   137

14 The Changing Seasons   147

Conclusion   159

Bibliography   169

Preface

In Herefordshire we have an annual event called "Spring Greens" where members of the various environmental organisations and networks across the County gather for a two day festival on the environment. There are talks and seminars, displays, music, and so on. It's not a religious event, even though many people of faith are involved, and I've always been challenged as a priest to articulate what distinctive contribution the Christian faith might bring to such a gathering.

Now I do not need to wonder any longer. As Christians, we have the ability to apply the ancient wisdom of scripture to the critical issues of today's environmental crises. The Bible itself is rooted in deep theological observation of the natural world, and this book unlocks understanding which, although always present in our sacred texts, has often been forgotten or ignored and which needs to be re-applied. There are a wealth of resources available to us, a great theological armoury that lies at our disposal as we wrestle with the future of our planet by listening to the wisdom that the planet itself provides for us.

After reading this book, I have far greater clarity of how to engage with my fellow environmentalists as we work together to protect and enhance our world.

Nick Read OBE FRAgS

Director, The Bulmer Foundation

Introduction

What the Donkey Saw

No room in the inn, of course,
And not that much in the stable,
What with the shepherds, Magi, Mary,
Joseph, the heavenly host—
Not to mention the baby
Using our manger as a cot.
You couldn't have squeezed another cherub in
For love nor money.

Still, in spite of the overcrowding,
I did my best to make them feel wanted.
I could see the baby and I
Would be going places together.

U A Fanthorpe[1]

U A Fanthorpe's poem imagines how the birth of Christ might have looked from a donkey's point of view. There is, of course, no mention of a donkey or a stable in the Biblical account but we like to think that a donkey was there and that it didn't

1. *New and Collected Poems*, London: Enitharmon, 2010.

complain too loudly when its quarters were gate-crashed and its meal container commandeered for a cot. According to Fanthorpe, the donkey welcomed the interlopers because it could foresee a useful partnership developing with the baby as he grew up, culminating perhaps in a joint triumphant entrance into the capital city. Behind the humour, however, lies a profound truth: that we human beings share this planet with other life forms and that they too are involved in God's saving activity. We are told that God's desire is, "...to bring *all things* in heaven and on earth together under one head, even Christ."[2]

When Job was struggling to make sense of the extreme weather events that had wreaked such social and economic devastation on his life, he found the narrow, over-simplistic viewpoint of his three friends unhelpful. His response was to advise them to,

> "...ask the animals, and they will teach you, or the birds of the air, and they will tell you; or speak to the earth, and it will teach you, or let the fish of the sea inform you. Which of all these does not know that the hand of the Lord has done this? In his hand is the life of every creature and the breath of all humankind."[3]

The idea that animals can have something important to say to human beings is found in many parts of the Bible. The author of Proverbs challenges the lazy with the words, "Go to the ant, you sluggard: consider its ways and be wise!"[4] Jeremiah asks why the Israelites can't obey the laws of God just as storks, doves, swifts and thrushes obey the laws of migration.[5] And Jesus asks why, when we are tempted to

2. Ephesians 1:10 (italics added). All Bible references are taken from the New International Version, unless otherwise stated.
3. Job 12:7-10
4. Proverbs 6:6
5. Jeremiah 8:7

worry about food, drink or clothing, we don't, "look at the birds of the air: they do not sow or reap or store away in barns, and yet your heavenly Father feeds them!"[6] He also refers to a hen gathering chicks under her wings and sheep recognising their master's voice as illustrations of how God loves us like a mother and guides us like a shepherd.[7]

As well as encouraging his friends to "ask the animals," Job tells them to "speak to the earth" indicating that wisdom can also be gained from the *inanimate* elements of creation, and certainly the Bible gives many examples of God and Jesus using different features of the natural world as vehicles for their message.[8] Like Job, we in the 21st century have been experiencing extreme weather events. The difference is that ours are part of a growing trend.[9] With runaway global warming and other human-inflicted ecological damage, the scale of the social and economic problems facing our world is massive. We therefore have all the more reason to pay attention to Job's advice.

This book began life as a series of sermons preached between April and August 2012 to a Baptist church in Gloucester, UK. Although a number of members shared a concern for the environment and some of these were already individually active within movements like the Green Party and Transition Gloucester, the fellowship as a whole had not engaged in an exploration of the subject. This situation did not feel right. How could we join together to worship the Creator and not be alarmed about the damage being done to His creation? How could we proclaim the Kingdom of God and not be concerned about the impact the ecological crisis was

6. Matthew 6:26
7. Luke 13:34; John 10:3-5
8. For example: trees (Genesis 12:6-7), stars (Genesis 15:5), bushes (Exodus 3:2-6), volcanoes (Exodus 19:18), branches (Jeremiah 1:11-12), wild flowers and grass (Luke 12:27-28), fig trees (Mark 13:28-29), water (John 4:13-14), etc.
9. *The Global Climate 2001-2010, A Decade of Climate Extremes*, World Meteorological Organisation. http://bit.ly/18vrBix

having on issues of compassion, justice, beauty and diversity? So, a working group was established to devise a church environment policy together with an action plan that would ensure both the policy's implementation and the church's accreditation as an "eco-congregation."[10] The sermon series was part of that action plan.

The intention was to make theological connections between the teachings of scripture and the realities of the global situation, so that people heard something that was both thoughtful and practical. In revising the material for this book, I decided to follow Job's advice and allow the voices of animals and natural features to shape the themes discussed. The chapters in Part One allow us to listen and respond to these voices while those in Part Two offer a way to live more balanced lives in harmony with nature's rhythms. Since the current ecological situation requires more than intellectual understanding, I have drawn on the insights of poets and artists. Their ability to touch the emotions can help the voices of nature found in Scripture to echo much more deeply within our lives and so provoke the desire to respond with action. This is crucial if the Gospel, which seeks through Christ to reconcile to God "*all things... on* earth,"[11] is to come, "not simply with words, but also with power, with the Holy Spirit and with deep conviction."[12]

10. Eco-congregation is an award scheme to encourage environmental awareness and action among churches. It is now administered by A Rocha.
11. Colossians 1:20
12. 1 Thessalonians 1:5

Part I

Listening to the Voices

The Beaten Donkey

Numbers 22:22–33

But God was very angry when he went, and the angel of the Lord stood in the road to oppose him. Balaam was riding on his donkey, and his two servants were with him. When the donkey saw the angel of the Lord standing in the road with a drawn sword in his hand, it turned off the road into a field. Balaam beat it to get it back on the road. Then the angel of the Lord stood in a narrow path through the vineyards, with walls on both sides. When the donkey saw the angel of the Lord, it pressed close to the wall, crushing Balaam's foot against it. So he beat the donkey again. Then the angel of the Lord moved on ahead and stood in a narrow place where there was no room to turn, either to the right or to the left. When the donkey saw the angel of the Lord, it lay down under Balaam, and he was angry and beat it with his staff.

Then the Lord opened the donkey's mouth, and it said to Balaam, "What have I done to you to make you beat me these three times? … Am I not your own donkey, which you have always ridden, to this day? Have I been in the habit of doing this to you?" "No," he said.

Then the Lord opened Balaam's eyes, and he saw the angel of the Lord standing in the road with his sword drawn. So he bowed low and fell face down. The angel of the Lord asked him, "Why have you beaten your donkey these three times? I have come here to oppose you because your path is a reckless one before me. The donkey saw me and turned away from me these three times. If it had not turned away, I would certainly have killed you by now, but I would have spared it."

Elegy for the Giant Tortoises

Let others pray for the passenger pigeon
the dodo, the whooping crane, the eskimo:
everyone must specialize.

I will confine myself to a meditation
upon the giant tortoises
withering finally on a remote island.

I concentrate in subway stations,
in parks, I can't quite see them,
they move to the peripheries of my eyes

but on the last day they will be there;
already the event
like a wave travelling shapes vision:

on the road where I stand they will materialise,
plodding past me in a straggling line
awkward without water

their small heads pondering
from side to side, their useless armour
sadder than tanks and history,

in their closed gaze ocean and sunlight paralysed,
lumbering up the steps, under the archways
toward the square glass altars

where the brittle gods are kept,
the relics of what we have destroyed,
our holy and obsolete symbols.

Margaret Atwood[1]

---

1. *Selected Poems 1965-1975*, Boston: Houghton Mifflin, 1976.

The rather strange episode of the talking donkey described in Numbers 22 occurred during the time when the Israelites were trekking through the wilderness towards the Promised Land. In the previous chapter, they had managed to defeat the armies of two local Kings—Sihon and Og. The Israelites hadn't been looking for trouble. In fact, they had sent a polite message to each of the kings seeking permission to travel across their territory and promising not to touch anything on their way through; but they were still attacked. The Israelites won the battles and carried on with their journey until they reached the borders of Moab.

Given the experience of his colleagues, the King of Moab was naturally rather anxious. He realized he couldn't defeat these Israelites without some kind of supernatural help, so he sent a delegation of nobles to request the services of a famous holy man called Balaam. These nobles arrived at Balaam's door and offered him a large sum of money if he would accompany them back to Moab the next day and place a curse on the Israelites. However, during the night, Balaam heard God tell him he shouldn't go, because God wanted these Israelites blessed, not cursed. When the nobles returned to Moab with news of Balaam's refusal, the King immediately sent another delegation made up of even more distinguished nobles and empowered them to offer Balaam even more money. Despite knowing that God had forbidden him to go, Balaam was so entranced by all the promised wealth, he said to the nobles, "I'll tell you what; stay the night and I'll just check to make sure." Balaam was clearly hoping he could change God's mind, and by the end of the night he had managed to convince himself that he'd heard God say, "Oh, all right then; you can go."

Balaam's love of money had so dulled his spiritual senses that he couldn't see the angel of the Lord standing in the road ahead of him, sword in hand. The *donkey* saw the angel and did its best to keep Balaam from being hacked to pieces. Instead of being grateful for the animal's warning, Balaam ended up beating it with his stick. At this point, God gave the

5

donkey a human voice to challenge its master's behaviour, and Balaam's eyes were finally opened to see the terrible danger that he faced. The angel told him in no uncertain terms that had his four-legged friend not turned away, he would certainly have been killed. In other words, the man was saved from destruction by listening to the aggrieved voice of an animal.

Why was it that Balaam had been completely oblivious to the presence of the sword-wielding angel poised to cut him down? The New Testament writers put it down to greed. According to Peter, Balaam "loved the wages of wickedness"[2] while Jude describes his error as a "rush for profit."[3] This was a man who had a faith in God, and yet allowed the prospect of increased prosperity to blind his eyes to the dangers that lay ahead. Even worse than that, this was a man who was prepared to allow *other people to suffer* merely to gain wealth for himself. His material blessing would have come as a direct result of a whole nation being cursed. What an awful man! And yet, if Nathan the prophet was standing in our churches today, he would turn to us and say, "*You* are that man!"[4]

We, along with the rest of our society, are blindly travelling towards destruction. We pollute our atmosphere, destroy our environment, clear our forests, drive plant and animal species to extinction, and consume oil and gas at a rate that cannot be sustained; and yet we seem to be oblivious to the dangers that await us along this road. Like Balaam, our blindness is caused by our affluence. The desire for material prosperity prevents us from seeing the sword-wielding angel. But it's worse than that. Like Balaam, we seem willing to allow *other people to suffer* in order for our comfortable lifestyle to be maintained. The wealth we enjoy in our more prosperous part of the world is at least partly the result of other nations being cursed—cursed with unfair trading arrangements that ensure their exports cannot compete with ours; cursed with being

2. 2 Peter 2:15–16
3. Jude v11
4. 2 Samuel 12:7

bullied by multinational companies who exploit their natural resources without proper recompense or care; cursed with the terrible effects of a warming climate and an economic recession that they did little to create. Balaam was willing to curse the poor, homeless Israelites in order to secure his own material prosperity. Are we in the 21st century all that different? As Christians, Jesus calls us to pronounce a *blessing* on the poor, not a curse. He wants us to join him in saying, "Blessed are you who are poor, for yours is the kingdom of God. Blessed are you who hunger now, for you will be satisfied."[5] And then, he wants us to join him in doing something to make that blessing a reality.

This will involve learning to see our modern world from a different perspective. We will need to go back to the very beginning to explore what God originally intended when he created the earth, its plants and creatures, and us. What values did he want human beings to have; what rights and responsibilities? We must also critically examine the road on which we are currently travelling—as individuals, as a church, and as a society—to see whether there is indeed a sword-wielding angel standing before us. We need to engage in some honest self-appraisal and maybe the animals are God's gift to help us do this. Maybe, like Balaam's donkey, they can be messengers from God to warn us of danger.

It was only in 1986 that a decision was finally made to replace the two hundred canaries being used in British coal mines with hand-held electronic detectors.[6] For decades, these small birds had accompanied miners underground. Being particularly sensitive to carbon monoxide gas which is colourless, odourless and tasteless to humans, the death throes of the canaries acted as a warning of its poisonous presence. Like the erratic behaviour of Balaam's donkey, the reactions of these birds revealed how close the miners were to the

5. Luke 6:20–21
6. http://bit.ly/1acVQwu ("UK Coal Mining Facts", DiscoveryUK.com)

sword-wielding angel of death. Even though the underground canaries have now been relieved of their duties, there are other birds that fulfil the role of "avian sentinel" on a larger scale—warning of environmental dangers that we humans have either not noticed or not taken seriously. Sometimes they raise the alarm through a decline in their own numbers. For example, we may like to sing about two turtle doves every Christmas[7] but, according to the recently published report *The State of Nature*,[8] the number of turtle doves in Britain has fallen by 93% since 1970. Worse still, some birds raise the alarm through their own extinction.

Figure 1 on the facing page shows a photograph of Todd McGrain's sculpture of a great auk. He created it as part of The Lost Bird Project,[9] an attempt to immortalise in bronze five species of North American birds that have been driven to extinction. According to McGrain,

> "The sculpture actually faces [Newfoundland's] Funk Islands, which were the last North American roosting sites of the great auk, and it's also the site of the most dramatic destruction of the population. It's where so many birds were taken to supply feathers for the feather trade in Europe."[10]

The inclusion of a ship in the background of the photograph adds a slightly sinister feel, given the role that sea-faring trade played in the bird's extinction in the 1840s. Also, the sculpture is the size of a man, which, combined with its upright posture, makes it resemble a lone human sentry keeping watch across

---

7. They appear in the carol *The Twelve Days of Christmas*.
8. http://bit.ly/18gjaos ("The State of Nature", RSPB, May 2013.)
9. See also htp://thelostbirdproject.tumblr.com/. The story of how Mc-Grain managed to erect these sculptures in the locations where these birds were last seen in the wild is the subject of a documentary film, selected in 2012 for the 30th International Festival of Films on Art in Montreal. (http://www.lostbirdfilm.org/)
10. http://bit.ly/1cxa8Wm ("Extinct bird immortalized in N.L.", *CBC News*)

Figure 1: Todd McGrain "The Great Auk". Bronze sculpture, Fogo Island, Newfoundland.

the Arctic for danger. Maybe that's what we should be doing, given that the melting of the Arctic ice has often been referred to as the "canary in the coal mine" of climate change.[11]

In a tragic echo of the beating that Balaam inflicted on his donkey, the last great auk to be seen alive in the British Isles was beaten to death by residents of St. Kilda in 1840 because they superstitiously believed it to be the cause of a storm they were suffering at the time. It is sobering to realize that the extinction of that bird prefigured the later "extinction" of the entire St Kilda community. In 1930, the last remaining 36 individuals were evacuated to the mainland.[12] It would be naïve to make a causal connection between the fate of the great auk and that of the islanders ninety years later. However, the two events can still serve as a kind of morality tale for our modern world, which is witnessing an increasing rate of species extinction caused by human activity.[13]

The poem *Elegy for the Giant Tortoises* by the Canadian novelist Margaret Atwood was first published in 1968 at a time when the damage that human beings were doing to the natural world first became big news. It refers to those great lumbering tortoises that live on the Galapagos Islands. The word "galapagos" is Spanish for "tortoise" and it seemed to the first Spanish explorers a fitting name to give to islands that were teeming with these creatures (about 5000, it is estimated). However, due to a long history of tortoise hunting, shortly after Margaret Atwood wrote her poem, their numbers were down to just fifteen.[14] Thankfully, since the 1970s, there's been a remarkable turnaround, with tortoises being bred in

11. http://bit.ly/P2xsy (*Arctic Sea Ice*, NRDC); http://bit.ly/1jlkjUV ("Arctic Sea Ice Gone in Summer Within Five Years?", *National Geographic*)
12. http://bit.ly/1clZq8N ("St Kilda: On the street where we lived", *The Guardian*)
13. http://bit.ly/1clZq8Q ("Humans driving extinction faster than species can evolve, say experts", *The Guardian*)
14. http://dailym.ai/1clZq8R ("On the road to recovery: Darwin's Galapagos tortoise threatened with extinction now number more than 1,000", *Daily Mail*)

captivity and re-introduced to the islands in increasing numbers. However, since other species have not been so fortunate and since there is still no sign of our human race changing course, we need to allow Atwood's giant tortoises to speak to us—to question our behaviour, just as the donkey did Balaam's.

Balaam received a warning through a donkey before it was almost clubbed to death; Margaret Atwood received a warning through a giant tortoise before it was almost hunted to extinction. The tortoise, however, was much further away from us than the donkey was to Balaam; it was "withering finally on a remote island". Like many of our world's environmental problems, it was happening so far away that it would have been easy for a Westerner to ignore it. Thankfully, Atwood didn't ignore it. Even though it was difficult, she imagined the tortoises as part of *her world*—"I concentrate in subway stations, in parks, I can't quite see them, they move to the peripheries of my eyes". And *we* need to imagine these and other animals as part of *our* world, because they *are* part of our world; we are all part of *God's* world. But, if we're not careful, those giant tortoises and many other endangered species will end up joining the great auk as just a few dusty exhibits in a museum. This is what Atwood dramatically visualizes—the tortoises themselves climbing up the steps of the National History Museum, resigned to taking their place inside some glass display cabinet. Is that what we want, asks Atwood? To see "giant tortoises... plodding past [us] in a straggling line / awkward without water / their small heads pondering / from side to side....lumbering up the steps, under the archways / toward the square glass altars / where the brittle gods are kept / the relics of what we have destroyed / our holy and obsolete symbols"?

Balaam's donkey and Atwood's tortoise both speak to us about our behaviour towards creation. They tell us that if we carry on wielding the stick against them, as Balaam did, we risk the angel wielding the sword against us. If we continue to destroy nature, we'll end up being destroyed ourselves. It's as if the earth itself is speaking through Balaam's donkey in verses 28-30. It's saying to us: "What have I done to you? Why have you exploited me so much? Am I not the same earth on which you have lived all your life?" We need to hear those accusations because they echo the voice of the Creator himself. Our materialistic, consumer lifestyle has become the idol at whose altar we are sacrificing the plants, animals and landscapes that God gave us to enjoy and care for. As the old hymn by C F Alexander (who also wrote *All Things Bright and Beautiful*) puts it: "Jesus calls us *from* the worship of the vain world's golden store, from each idol that would keep us, saying, 'Christian, love me more'."[15]

---

15. 'Jesus calls o'er the tumult', No. 359, *Complete Mission Praise*, London: Harper Collins, 2005.

The Protective Tree

Daniel 4:10–16

These are the visions I saw while lying in bed: I looked, and there before me stood a tree in the middle of the land. Its height was enormous. The tree grew large and strong and its top touched the sky; it was visible to the ends of the earth. Its leaves were beautiful, its fruit abundant, and on it was food for all. Under it the wild animals found shelter, and the birds lived in its branches; from it every creature was fed.

In the visions I saw while lying in bed, I looked, and there before me was a holy one, a messenger, coming down from heaven. He called in a loud voice: "Cut down the tree and trim off its branches; strip off its leaves and scatter its fruit. Let the animals flee from under it and the birds from its branches. But let the stump and its roots, bound with iron and bronze, remain in the ground, in the grass of the field.

"Let [the king] be drenched with the dew of heaven, and let him live with the animals among the plants of the earth. Let his mind be changed from that of a man and let him be given the mind of an animal, till seven times pass by for him."

Luke 12:42–46

The Lord answered, "Who then is the faithful and wise manager, whom the master puts in charge of his servants to give them their food allowance at the proper time? It will be good for that servant whom the master finds doing so when he returns. I tell you the truth, he will put him in charge of all his possessions. But suppose the servant says to himself, 'My master is taking a long time in coming,' and he then begins to beat the menservants and maidservants, and to eat and drink and get drunk. The master of that servant will come on a day when he does not expect him and at an hour he is not aware of. He will cut him to pieces and assign him a place with the unbelievers.

Genesis 1:26–30

Then God said, "Let us make mankind in our image, in our likeness, so that they may rule over the fish in the sea and the birds in the sky, over the livestock and all the wild animals, and over all the creatures that move along the ground."

> So God created mankind in his own image,
>   in the image of God he created them;
>   male and female he created them.

God blessed them and said to them, "Be fruitful and increase in number; fill the earth and subdue it. Rule over the fish in the sea and the birds in the sky and over every living creature that moves on the ground." Then God said, "I give you every seed-bearing plant on the face of the earth and every tree that has fruit with seed in it...and to all the beasts of the earth and all the birds of the air and all the creatures that move on the ground—everything that has the breath of life in it—I give every green plant for food." And it was so.

The last chapter featured a man being told off for beating his donkey with a stick. This one begins with a man being told off for beating his fellow human beings. Jesus' parable in Luke 12 spells out the difference between the faithful and unfaithful manager. The unfaithful manager takes advantage of his master's prolonged absence and, "begins to beat the menservants and maidservants, and to eat and drink and get drunk" (v45). He had been put "...in charge of [the] servants to give them their food allowance at the proper time" (v42), but instead, he mistreats the other members of the household and devours all the food and drink himself. This man failed to be a good steward of the people and the provisions that his master had placed in his charge.

King Nebuchadnezzar was warned about behaving in a similar fashion in Daniel 4. The message came through a vision of an enormous tree whose protective canopy provided food and shelter for all the wild animals and birds. That tree challenged Nebuchadnezzar to do the same for all those living under his rule. If he chose instead to act like the unfaithful manager in Jesus' parable, God would remove from him not just the privilege of being a king, but the privilege of being a human being. "Let his mind be changed from that of a man and let him be given the mind of an animal" (v16). In other words, God used the image of the protective tree to define for Nebuchadnezzar what having power and authority should look like.

This is an image that each one of us must take note of because all of humanity has been placed in a position of power over the rest of creation. In Genesis 1 God declares his intention that human beings should rule over the earth and all its life forms (v26), and that he has provided an abundance of green plants for the world's creatures to eat (v30). It's clear that human beings were being given a stewardship role, like the manager in Jesus' parable, to ensure that all living things received their food "at the proper time." Has humanity been faithful in carrying out this task? Or have we said to ourselves, "[our] master is taking a long time in coming" and begun mistreating the other creatures and devouring all the available food and drink ourselves? The evidence we see around us today suggests that the human race is acting more like the *unfaithful* servant in Jesus' parable than the faithful one.

A provocative article was written by Lynn White in the March 1967 edition of the journal *Science*.[1] It was entitled *The Historical Roots of our Ecological Crisis* and it placed much of the blame for the problems facing the environment on the Jewish and Christian traditions. White claimed that, unlike pagan religions which showed great respect for the natural world, Christianity in particular had encouraged people to believe that nature existed for no other purpose but to serve human requirements. And it's true that the divine mandate in Genesis 1 to rule over all other living things has been understood by many to give humanity permission—encouragement even—to exploit the earth for its own ends and desires. But this was not the original intention of Genesis 1.

The statement in v26, "let them rule...", comes immediately after the statement, "let us make man *in our image, in our likeness.*" These two statements are tied and must be understood together. God only gives human beings authority to rule because they are made in his own image and likeness. He wants them to rule *as he does*, the One in whose image and likeness they are created. So, the question that needs asking is this: how does *God* rule over his creation, and how can we, his stewards or managers, follow his example? The answer to that question can be summed up in three words: hospitality, honour and hope.

Hospitality

An 8th century Greek theologian called John of Damascus described the Creation as God "*making room*" for things to exist alongside Him. This lovely thought has been amplified by the modern scholar Robert Jenson, who wrote: "For God to create is for him to *open a place* in his triune life for others

1. *Science*, 155(3767), March 10, 1967, pp. 1203–1207.

than the three whose mutual life he is."[2] In other words, creation is an act of divine hospitality.

We can see this from the way the land, the sea, the plants and the animals are not so much ordered to appear, as invited. Each time something is created in Genesis 1, the command of God is expressed as: "*let* there be light...*let* the water be filled...*let* the air be filled...*let* the earth produce." The expression in Hebrew conveys the idea that God is giving permission for each new thing to come into existence. It's as if they are appearing in his embryonic world as a guest. And to make the newly arrived animals feel at home, God prepares a banquet for them: "for all the wild animals and for all the birds I have provided grass and leafy plants for food" (v30). *This* is what it means to "rule" in the image and likeness of God; it means to welcome, to provide for, to watch over—just as a protective tree welcomes, provides for and watches over the animals and birds that live within and beneath its branches.

Maybe that's why, a few chapters later, God was so impressed with Noah. Just think of the hospitality Noah and his family were willing to show to God's creation inside the ark! Within that small wooden craft they had to make room for so many different creatures, each with their own needs and requirements. Just as God had done in Creation, Noah provided all the animals and birds with food and shelter. Imagine how much thought and sensitivity would have been required to make each creature feel at home in that ark. And when you look at photographs of the earth taken from space, our planet looks a bit like an ark, floating in a sea of blackness. It takes a lot of thought and sensitivity to ensure all the members of our global household feel at home, but that's what it means to be good stewards. That's what it means to rule in the image and likeness of God; to offer hospitality.

2. Quoted in Norman Wirzba, *The Paradise of God,* Oxford: Oxford University Press, 2003, p. 19.

Honour

At the end of each day, we are told that God looked at everything he had created and declared it "good." By saying this, God was giving honour to every object and every creature. He was affirming that they were good not only in their appearance, but also in their existence, since their very being was evidence of the good and perfect will of God. God thought very highly of this material world—so highly, in fact, that he was willing to become part of it himself through the flesh-and-blood body of Jesus Christ.

Unfortunately, Christianity became infected in its early centuries by two unhelpful influences that caused many believers to look down on the physical. The first was the work of Plato who claimed that the only thing that was truly real was the invisible world of eternal forms, and that what we see around us in this physical world is just an inferior copy. The second damaging influence came from Gnosticism, a movement which claimed that this material world wasn't just inferior, it was actually *evil*. The effect of these ideas was to tempt many Christians to look down on their physical bodies and on their material surroundings, and believe that the only thing that really mattered was their invisible soul and the spiritual world that exists beyond this one. They saw this life as merely a training ground for the next life; a launch-pad for heaven. If this earth was going to be discarded one day like an old suit or a butterfly's cocoon, then why bother worrying about how tatty or damaged it became?

My church used to hold a monthly "Hard Questions Group" and one of its meetings discussed the idea of beauty. Should we spend money on our homes to make them beautiful; or should we be content with utility? There was an assumption that the spiritual activity that goes on within a home is more important than the physical surroundings in which it takes place. Why spend money on replacing a sofa that is stained or a carpet that is threadbare when it's the spiritual and emotional life that really counts? We should instead give the money to the poor.[3]

But then we realized that our physical surroundings are actually *part* of our spiritual and emotional life. Our sofa, our carpet, our pictures, create a sense of belonging. They make us and our guests feel at home; they communicate our values and tastes ("She has done a beautiful thing to me"[4]). A tatty house could say to our family or our guests, "I don't care enough about you to make an effort." A broken, draughty window can say, "I don't consider your health or your safety to be all that important."

The same is true for this physical world—which is also our home. We may sympathise with the old gospel song that says, "This world is *not* my home; I'm just a-passing through / My treasures are laid up somewhere beyond the blue," but those lyrics are misleading. The desire of the songwriter to give struggling people hope that the next life will free them from the sufferings of this one is very laudable, but that doesn't mean this world is not our home. Of course it's our home—we live here! It's also home to countless animals and plants. Our physical well-being is dependent on this earth, and so too is our spiritual and emotional well-being.

Maybe, as well as being our home, the earth is also our mother. Genesis 1 tells us that we were created by the spoken word of Father God; but Genesis 2 goes on to tell us that we were also created from the body of the earth. We were formed from its soil. God gave us life, but the earth gave us birth. The word "nature" itself comes from the Latin meaning "birth." So, in that sense, we have both a Father God and a mother nature, and we are told in the fifth commandment to, "Honour your father and mother; that your days may be long on the earth."

3. The comment made about the woman who anointed Jesus in Bethany, Mark 14:5.
4. Jesus' response to the woman in Mark 14:6.

Hope

Worried by the implications of Plato's teaching that God created the world from material that was already there, the Early Church put forward the doctrine that the universe was made *from nothing*. It is an important doctrine because it underlines the truth that God was the origin of everything that exists ("through him all things were made; without him nothing was made that has been made."[5])

Having said this, the opening words of the Bible are rather ambiguous: "In the beginning, God created the heavens and the earth. Now the earth was formless and empty, darkness was over the surface of the deep, and the Spirit of God was hovering over the waters."[6] The mention of a formless, empty earth, a dark surface, and waters, sounds like there was material already there for God to work with. Maybe it was material he had created earlier, in preparation for his magnum opus! The advantage of acknowledging this pre-existing matter, however, is that it gives us *hope*. It points to a God who can take something that is formless and empty and give it order and beauty; a God who can take dark waters and transform them with his peace and light. Isn't this the hope of the Gospel? Isn't this what keeps us going—the hope that there is no mess in our lives so big that God can't fix; no night so dark that God can't illuminate; no situation so bleak that God can't rejuvenate?

It also gives us hope in our present ecological crisis. Sometimes all the news about global warming and environmental destruction can seem completely overwhelming. We feel we are at the mercy of powerful climatic and economic forces beyond our control. And yet, when we read Genesis 1, we see a God who was able to create a good and beautiful world out of chaos, darkness, and raging ocean. Surely that God is just as able to *re*-create a good and beautiful world out

5. John 1:3
6. Genesis 1:1–2

of the chaos, darkness, and rising sea levels that we might cause. This doesn't mean that we can just ignore the problems and carry on as we are; that wouldn't be good stewardship.[7] "The faithful and wise manager," said Jesus, is the one who his master can put in charge of his servants and know that he/she will "give them their food allowance at the proper time." The manager's rule, in other words, should be exercised in the image and likeness of his master's rule—characterized by hospitality, honour and hope. *That* is the calling God places upon you and me. It's a tough challenge. We feel the weakness of our efforts; but from a small seed can come a large protective tree, "with such big branches that the birds of the air can perch in its shade."[8]

---

7. The use of the term "stewardship" has been criticised by some scholars for being hierarchical, vague and over-confident—it assumes that we have the necessary knowledge and wisdom. See Richard Bauckham, *Bible and Ecology*, London: Darton, Longman & Todd, 2010.
8. Mark 4:32

The Humble Soil

Genesis 2:4–17

This is the account of the heavens and the earth when they were created, when the Lord God made the earth and the heavens. Now no shrub had yet appeared on the earth and no plant had yet sprung up, for the Lord God had not sent rain on the earth and there was no one to work the ground, but streams came up from the earth and watered the whole surface of the ground. Then the Lord God formed a man from the dust of the ground and breathed into his nostrils the breath of life, and the man became a living being.

Now the Lord God had planted a garden in the east, in Eden; and there he put the man he had formed. The Lord God made all kinds of trees grow out of the ground—trees that were pleasing to the eye and good for food. In the middle of the garden were the tree of life and the tree of the knowledge of good and evil…

…The Lord God took the man and put him in the Garden of Eden to work it and take care of it. And the Lord God commanded the man, "You are free to eat from any tree in the garden; but you must not eat from the tree of the knowledge of good and evil, for when you eat from it you will certainly die."

Philippians 2:6–8

Who, being in very nature God,
    did not consider equality with God something to be
        grasped; but made himself nothing,
taking the very nature of a servant,
    being made in human likeness.
And being found in appearance as a man,
    he humbled himself and became obedient to death—
        even death on a cross!

God's Grandeur

The world is charged with the grandeur of God.
    It will flame out, like shining from shook foil;
    It gathers to a greatness, like the ooze of oil
Crushed. Why do men then now not reck his rod?
Generations have trod, have trod, have trod;
    And all is seared with trade; bleared, smeared with toil;

    And wears man's smudge and shares man's smell: the
        soil
Is bare now, nor can foot feel, being shod.
And for all this, nature is never spent;
    There lives the dearest freshness deep down things;
And though the last lights off the black West went
    Oh, morning, at the brown brink eastward, springs—
Because the Holy Ghost over the bent
    World broods with warm breast and with ah! bright
        wings.

Gerard Manley Hopkins[1]

---

1. *The poems of Gerard Manley Hopkins*, Oxford: Oxford University Press, 1967.

Genesis 1 may have placed humanity at the pinnacle of creation with power over everything else; but Genesis 2 brings us back down to earth—literally! In v7, we're told that God made human beings out of the earth—the very same earth he had used to make all the other animals in v19. Later in chapter 3, a chastened Adam and Eve would hear these sobering words: "You will go back to the soil from which you were formed. You were made from soil, and you will become soil again" (v19 GNB).

This human connection with the soil is further underlined by the actual name given to the man. He is called "Adam" which is very close to the word "adamah," meaning arable land or soil. The writer is telling us that underneath all of our posturing and pride, we are simply *earth*lings—animated columns of moulded soil! This verbal link has been preserved in our own language where the word "human" comes from the same Latin root as the word "humus" meaning soil. And "humus" is also the source of the word "humility". The soil, therefore, speaks to us about being humble in our attitude towards other living things. "God knows what we are made of; he remembers that we are dust"[2]—we need to remember it too. The soil also speaks to us about death-embracing service, because the soil is the place where dead matter is received and transformed into new life. If the soil was not present to perform this recycling, purifying role, there would be no life on planet earth. It therefore acts as a servant to all the plants and animals.

This servant nature of the soil was embodied in the life of Jesus. We read in Philippians 2 that Jesus allowed himself to be "made in human likeness" (v7). This was partly because men and women, despite being created in the likeness of *God*, had failed to reflect that likeness in their lives. So Jesus took on *human* likeness in order to show us how *God's likeness* shines out from a human life through *servant-hood.* We are told that Jesus took "the very nature of a servant;" and "humbled

---

2. Psalm 103:14

himself and became obedient to death..." (v8). It is *this* soil-like attitude that *we* should have, writes Paul in v5; the attitude of a *servant —humble* and *obedient*.

However, Jesus' servant role wasn't limited just to humanity; he actually came to serve the *whole* of creation. We are told by Paul that, "Through the Son, God decided to bring the *whole universe* back to himself. God made peace through his Son's sacrificial death on the cross and so brought back to himself *all things, both on earth and in heaven.*"[3] He also describes, "all of creation" longing to be "set free from its slavery to decay," so that it can "...share the glorious freedom of the children of God."[4] In other words, Jesus came to serve the *whole of creation* through his humility and obedience, and in doing so, perfectly fulfilled the original vocation that had been given to men and women in Genesis 2.

That original vocation begins in v5, where an absence of plants on the earth is attributed to a lack of rain and a lack of anyone "to cultivate the land". God immediately remedies these two deficiencies by providing a stream to water the garden (vs. 10–14) and a human being "to cultivate and guard it" (v7, 15). However, the Hebrew word translated as "cultivate" in vs. 5 and 15 also means "*serve*". Verse 15 can therefore be read as follows, "Then the Lord God placed the man in the Garden of Eden *to serve it and guard it.*" This servant role was to be demonstrated through humility and obedience.

Humility

In Greek legend, there was a powerful giant called Antaeus, the son of Poseidon (the god of the sea) and Gaia (the goddess of the earth). Antaeus lived in Libya and challenged everyone

3. Colossians 1:20 GNB (italics added)
4. Romans 8:19–23 GNB

travelling through his territory to a wrestling match—which he always won. The reason he always won was because he drew his great strength *from the earth* (his mother). One day, Hercules turned up. During the course of the ensuing wrestling match, Hercules noticed that every time he threw Antaeus down on the ground, his muscles immediately swelled up and he was able to leap up with renewed energy. Hercules worked out that it was contact with the earth that gave Antaeus his power; so the next time he had hold of him, he lifted him clean off his feet. Without being able to touch the ground, Antaeus' strength slowly drained away and Hercules was able to crush him to death.

Maybe there's a sense in which *our* strength drains away when we lose contact with the earth. Gerard Manley Hopkins clearly thought so. In his poem *God's Grandeur*, he says:

> Generations have trod, have trod, have trod;
>   And all is seared with trade; bleared, smeared
>   with toil;
>
>   And wears man's smudge and shares man's
>   smell: the soil
> Is bare now, nor can foot feel, being shod.

The barrier that our leather soles place between our feet and the soil is symptomatic of the barrier between our whole lives and creation caused by industrialisation and urbanisation. We walk on pavements or concrete, and we know very little about where our food comes from or how it is grown. Not only can our foot not feel, "being shod"; neither can our hearts feel, being so insulated from the natural world. And yet that natural world is, "charged with the grandeur of God. It will flame out, like shining from shook foil." Moses and Joshua discovered this; they encountered the grandeur of God on the Sinai mountain and in the Jordan valley. Their response was to unshod their feet. "Take off your sandals" said God, "because the place where you are standing is holy ground."[5] Maybe *we* need to be humble enough to acknowledge the presence of God within nature, and treat it much more like holy ground than we do. Maybe God would speak to us more clearly through his creation if only we would unshod our feet; if only we would draw close enough to hear his voice speaking through the wonder, the mystery and the beauty of what he has made.

Obedience

As a servant of creation, Adam also needed to be obedient to the instructions he was given.

1. He had to *care* for God's creation.

   "The Lord God placed the man in the Garden of Eden to serve it and guard it" (v15) and that involved *work*—digging, pruning, weeding, protecting young plants, repairing storm damage, moving animals around to prevent overgrazing, and so on. But God designed our bodies and our minds in such a way that we find such labour deeply fulfilling. We feel good when we are sweating away in the garden; we feel pleased when we have created a flower border or harvested some vegetables. There's a moving passage in Tolstoy's novel *Anna Karenin*, where the landowner Constantine Levin decides to join his workers in cutting down hay in one of his meadows.

   > "I must have some physical exercise, or my temper will certainly go to pieces" he thought, and determined to do some mowing, however awkward he might feel about it with his brother or the peasants.[6]

5. Exodus 3:5; Joshua 5:15
6. Tolstoy, *Anna Karenin*, London: Penguin Classics, 1954, p. 268.

So off he goes, and then we are told:

> In the very heat of the day, the mowing did not seem such hard work. The perspiration with which he was drenched cooled him, while the sun, that burned his back, his head, and his arms, bare to the elbow, gave a vigour and dogged energy to his labour; and more and more often now came those moments of oblivion, when it was possible not to think of what one was doing. The scythe cut of itself. Those were happy moments.[7]

Later that evening Levin bursts into his house, hair matted and clothes grimy.

> "We've done the whole meadow!" he cried joyfully. "Oh, it's so good! Marvellous! And how have you been getting on?" Levin had completely forgotten their disagreeable conversation of the previous day.[8]

Most people have had experiences like his. To be servants of creation is what we were made for; so it's not surprising that cultivating/serving and guarding our natural world seems to touch something deep inside of us.

2. Adam had to observe the limits that God had set.

In vs. 16–18, we are told that, "The Lord God commanded the man, 'You are free to eat from any tree in the garden, but you must not eat from the tree of the knowledge of good and evil, for when you eat of it you will surely die'." God was setting

7. Ibid, p. 273.
8. Ibid, p. 277.

out safety precautions to protect both humans and all of creation. They were allowed a huge amount of freedom, but still had to recognise that there was a limit to their understanding. They weren't God; they didn't know everything.

I sometimes take my puppet dog Rollo into a local infant school assembly and on one occasion told the children that Rollo was lucky to be alive because he had disobeyed the one instruction I had given him. I had told him that he was free to run around the local park as much as he wanted, chase any birds, dig any holes, but the *one thing he mustn't do* was go beyond the park boundary. Rollo didn't listen of course and ran straight out onto the road in front of a bus. Luckily, he escaped with just a few bruises!

To be a servant of creation is to respect limits. Our planet is finite; its resources aren't endless; its ability to recover from increased levels of destruction and pollution isn't guaranteed. It's true that Gerard Manley Hopkins finished his poem on an optimistic note. After lamenting that, "all is seared with trade; bleared, smeared with toil; and wears man's smudge and shares man's smell; the soil is bare now"...he comforts himself that, "for all this, nature is never spent". However, Hopkins was writing in 1877, eight years before Karl Benz invented the first motor car! The situation we face *today* looks far more precarious. Observing nature's limits is all the more crucial. Scientists talk about "tipping points", when habitats are pushed beyond their ability to recover. When too many trees are cleared from the rain forest, the unprotected soil gets washed away and the land becomes barren. There is general agreement that once global temperatures rise by more than 2 degrees centigrade, feedback loops will kick in that will make problems even worse.

As Christians, we must remain hopeful. If Hopkins could cling to his faith in God despite the negative effects of the industrialization he saw around him, so should we. If we carry out our *servant* responsibilities to the best of our ability, if we are *humble* towards God's creation and *obedient* in caring for it, then

"...though the last lights off the black West went
    Oh, morning, at the brown brink eastward,
       springs—
Because the Holy Ghost over the bent
    World broods with warm breast and with ah!
       bright wings."

The Devious Snake

Genesis 3:14–24

So the Lord God said to the serpent, "Because you have done this,

> Cursed are you above all livestock
>   and all wild animals!
> You will crawl on your belly
>   and you will eat dust
>   all the days of your life.
> And I will put enmity
>   between you and the woman,
>   and between your offspring and hers;
> he will crush your head,
>   and you will strike his heel."

To the woman he said,

> "I will greatly increase your pains in childbearing;
>   with painful labour you will give birth to children.
> Your desire will be for your husband,
>   and he will rule over you."

To Adam he said, "Because you listened to your wife and ate fruit from the tree about which I commanded you, 'You must not eat from it,'

> Cursed is the ground because of you;
>> through painful toil you will eat food from it
>> all the days of your life.
> It will produce thorns and thistles for you,
>> and you will eat the plants of the field.
> By the sweat of your brow
>> you will eat your food
> until you return to the ground,
>> since from it you were taken;
> for dust you are
>> and to dust you will return."

Adam named his wife Eve, because she would become the mother of all the living.

The Lord God made garments of skin for Adam and his wife and clothed them. And the Lord God said, "The man has now become like one of us, knowing good and evil. He must not be allowed to reach out his hand and take also from the tree of life and eat, and live forever." So the Lord God banished him from the Garden of Eden to work the ground from which he had been taken. After he drove the man out, he placed on the east side of the Garden of Eden cherubim and a flaming sword flashing back and forth to guard the way to the tree of life.

Fifty years ago, the great fear that gripped many people was the prospect of nuclear destruction. It was the era of the Cold War and the Cuban Missile Crisis, and the relationship between America and the Soviet Union was very tense. If things *had* got out of hand, we would probably not be here today. Nuclear destruction is instant, simple, external and indiscriminate. It is instant in the sense that the destruction would happen in a split second and we wouldn't know much about it. It is simple in the sense that it results from a President or General simply pressing a button or entering a launch code. It is external because it comes from forces outside of us and beyond our control. And it is indiscriminate because it has an equally devastating effect on everyone.

Today, the fear is not so much of nuclear destruction, as ecological destruction[1]; but the way we experience this fear is very different. Instead of an instant demise, we face a much more gradual one, as the environment slowly deteriorates. Instead of a simple result of missiles being launched, our ecological destruction is so complex that it's hard to understand. Even scientists aren't sure how much of our global warming is man-made and huge computers are needed to calculate the multiple interactions between atmosphere, oceans, vegetation and animal life. Also, instead of an external cause, ecological destruction is produced by something internal—our own inner addiction to a lifestyle of ever increasing material comfort and energy consumption, combined with rising global population. And unlike the indiscriminate suffering caused by a nuclear war, ecological destruction is discriminatory, in that it falls far more heavily on those people and nations that are already poor and struggling. So, because ecological destruction is gradual, complex, internal and (at the moment, at least) something mainly suffered by other people, it's difficult for us in the West to get very motivated about it.

In the last chapter, we noted God's warning to Adam: "You must not eat from the tree of the knowledge of good and evil, for when you eat of it you will surely die" (v17). On the face of it, this threat displays many of the characteristics of nuclear destruction. Disobedience would lead to a death that was instant ("when you eat"), simple (man disobeys God, God punishes man; end of story), and external (destruction comes from God, ie: from outside the man). And yet, when we read Genesis 3, we discover that after Adam and Eve had eaten the forbidden fruit, their death *wasn't* instant, but gradual. Although their rift with God caused immediate spiritual and

1. I owe the idea of comparing ecological destruction with nuclear destruction to Sallie McFague's *The Body of God*, London: SCM Press, 1993, pp. 1–2.

emotional damage, they still continued to live, physically, for many years. Neither could we describe the effects of their disobedience as "simple". The details of the different curses on the snake, the woman and the man have tested the brains of the best scholars for centuries. What are the complex images of speaking reptiles, increased birth pains, hard soil, and thorns supposed to mean? Also, the punishment is not so much *external* as *internal*. Adam and Eve were not vapourised by a flash of lightning coming from above. Instead, they were afflicted with pain, sorrow and frustration from within as their separation from God affected their self-image, relationships, and behaviour towards the natural world. In other words, what we see in Genesis 3 and beyond seems to mirror our own ecological crisis.

The crisis in Genesis 3 was caused by Adam and Eve's failure to exhibit the humility and obedience that should characterise those called to be *servants of creation*.[2] Instead of accepting their divinely allotted place in the world, they allowed their pride to be aroused by the snake's suggestion that the forbidden fruit would make them as wise as God (v5-6). And instead of being obedient and accepting the limits that God had placed on what they should take from the Garden, they became greedy. They saw, "that the fruit of the tree was good for food and pleasing to the eye, and also desirable for gaining wisdom" (v6), and they wanted it. In the place of humility and obedience, Adam and Eve displayed pride and greed. Both of these sinful attitudes were related to *their failure to observe limits*—the limit on how much they should exploit nature to bolster their own self-image, and the limit on how much they should consume nature to meet their own desires. As a consequence of this, they unleashed two tragic processes: escalation and expulsion.

2. See chapter 2.

Escalation

In v16, God says to Eve: "I will *increase* your pains in child-bearing." To use the word "increase" means that there must have been some level of trouble and pain involved already. The effect of Eve's disobedience was that this suffering would now escalate. Instead of being a modest amount of pain that hallowed the experience of creating a new life; it would become a distressing amount. It's as if God is saying, "If *you* are not willing to observe the limits I originally intended, then neither will the trouble and pain of childbirth observe the limits I originally intended."

The same theme of escalation is present in God's judgment of Adam. He tells him in v17: "Cursed is the ground because of you; through painful toil you will eat of it all the days of your life." Hard work itself is not the punishment, because Adam had already been doing that and finding it very fulfilling. He had, after all, been placed in the Garden of Eden with specific instructions "to work it and take care of it" (2:15). The difference now is the amount of effort it would require for him to grow what he needed to survive. God also mentions thorns and thistles (v18)—not that these didn't exist before Adam had sinned; it's just that now they would become more widespread and difficult to control.

This process of escalation, however, wasn't limited to birth-pains and manual work, it also affected relationships. Adam and Eve would have had their disagreements with God and with each other long before they ate the forbidden fruit; such differences are part of healthy relationships and their resolution helped to make those relationships stronger. However, after their rebellion, the level of disagreement escalated. Adam started by blaming Eve and God for his behaviour. "The woman *you* put here with me – she gave me some fruit... and I ate it" (v12). Soon God was predicting serious tensions between them, telling Eve: "your desire will be for your husband and he will rule over you" (v16).

Conflict within their family further escalated in Chapter 4 with the murder of one of their sons by the other, and by Chapter 6, we are told that the earth had become, "corrupt in God's sight and full of violence" (v11).

There was also an escalation in human disrespect for God. Adam and Eve's attempt to "be like God" was soon being replicated on a much larger scale by people claiming to be descended from human women and heavenly beings (6:1–4). People began acting as if they were as powerful as God, but because they didn't have God's wisdom or God's mercy, the result was disastrous not just for humanity but for all of creation.

We have seen this in recent history. The effects are vividly portrayed in Paul Nash's picture *We are making a new world*. (fig. 2 on the next page) Painted in 1918, it shows the aftermath of the Battle of Passchendaele; the muddy craters, the blasted tree trunks, the barren landscape. The impact of the picture lies in its colour and symbolism. The clouds that God created to bring refreshing rain to the earth are blood red; the mounds look like gravestones, and the shattered trees resemble human hands reaching up in desperation. The title of the painting sounds like it's been lifted from a modern advertising slogan. It mocks politicians, generals and technology for making grand claims about creating a better world.

The power of Nash's image is not limited to the memory of how the First World War reduced beautiful fields and woodlands to a lunar landscape; it also resonates with more recent photographs of Vietnamese forests stripped bare by Agent Orange and napalm, and of other forests being cleared at a worrying rate today for commercial profit. These and many other situations are caused by human beings thinking they are as wise as God and therefore don't have to worry about observing any limits to their power or their greed. The words "Cursed be the ground because of you," spoken to Adam in v17, could equally be spoken to many politicians and military chiefs. They should also ring in the ears of Union Carbide executives

Figure 2: Paul Nash—*We are making a new world.*

whose drive for profit over safety led to an explosion at their factory in Bhopal, India, that killed thousands of people and poisoned the local environment for years to come.

We too are in danger of hearing God say to us: "Cursed be the ground because of you," as our ever-increasing demand for higher living standards and consumer goods puts more and more strain on so many areas of the earth. The Hebrew word used here for 'curse' means *a barrier that prevents blessing.* Maybe our addiction to a high consumption, high energy, high waste lifestyle is a barrier that prevents the ground in many poor countries from enjoying God's blessing.

Expulsion

As well as unleashing a process of *escalation* into our world, Adam and Eve's pride and greed also resulted in expulsion. In v23, we read: "So the Lord God banished [Adam] from the Garden of Eden to work the ground from which he had been taken." God could no longer trust Adam and Eve to look after the garden as humble and obedient servants of his creation; so he expelled them into the more wild and overgrown land that lay beyond its boundary. In effect, God is saying, "Since you seem determined to live beyond my limits, you can go and live beyond the limits of my garden, and there you will see what it's like to be at the mercy of other people just as proud and greedy as you are."

Of course, an expulsion very similar to this did happen centuries later, when God drove his people out of the Promised Land into Babylonia where they did indeed have to live for seventy years at the mercy of those just as proud and greedy as they had been. In fact, some scholars think the Adam and Eve story was written as a parable about the Babylonian Exile.[3]

---

3. For example: Exeter University's Dr. Francesca Stavrakopoulou who details her theory in the third and final part of the 2011 BBC TV documentary series *The Bible's Buried Secrets.*

They claim that Solomon's Temple was the real Garden of Eden, being decorated as it was by carvings of all kinds of animals and plants. Instead of obeying God, the King of Judah was led astray by foreign wives, who brought into the temple the worship of other gods—one in the form of a snake. However, most agree it is more likely that the story of Adam and Eve was already in existence and became a resource to help the exiles gain a greater understanding of why they had been expelled from Canaan. As well as illustrating their own failure to be humble and obedient servants of God and his creation, this ancient story offered the exiles hope—for three reasons:

1. *The story showed them that God still cared for people however disobedient they were.*

   After God had passed judgment on the first couple, v21 says "the Lord God made garments of skin for Adam and his wife and clothed them." This would have encouraged the struggling exiles to hope that God would show a similar care for them.

2. *The story offered the hint that access to the Tree of Life wouldn't be denied forever.*

   When God told the snake in v15 that the woman's offspring would crush his head, the Hebrew word for 'offspring' (or 'seed') is singular. This gave the exiled Jews hope that an individual descendant of Eve would rise up to crush their enemies. One of their prophets had a vision of a new temple from which a river flowed to nourish many new trees of life: "Their leaves will not wither, nor will their fruit fail... their fruit will serve for food and their leaves for healing."[4]

3. *The story goes on to describe an ecologically friendly life.*

   In Noah, the exiles were able to see a person repairing some of the damage Adam and Eve had caused. According to Genesis 5:29, his father chose the name Noah because it meant 'comfort' and, "he will comfort us in the labour and painful toil of our

4. Ezekiel 47:12

41

hands caused by the ground the Lord has cursed." Despite the flood of violence and subsequent flood of water, Noah served God and his creation with humility and obedience, offering hospitality and care to all the plants, animals and birds inside the ark. He observed the limits that God had given for the safety of all that were aboard, and was neither proud nor greedy.

The Genesis story gives us who live in the twenty-first century hope as well. The God who cared for Adam and Eve despite their failings also cares for us despite the mess we seem to be making of his creation. We are able, with hindsight, to see that Jesus was the offspring of Eve who crushed the temptations of the snake. We saw him do it after forty days in the wilderness when he refused to exceed his Father's limits to gain food, fame and riches for himself. We see him doing it again in Revelation 20 where we're told his angel, "seized the dragon, that ancient serpent, who is the devil, or Satan, and bound him for a thousand years," after which "he was thrown into the lake of fire."[5]

In the first book of the Bible we read that Adam, "must not be allowed to reach out his hand and take from the tree of life and eat, and live for ever;"[6] but in the *last* book of the Bible we read that in the new Jerusalem there is a "tree of life, which bears fruit twelve times a year, once each month; and its leaves are for the healing of the nations."[7] That tree represents Jesus Christ, the ultimate source of God's life and healing.

Scientists are concerned that part of the West Antarctic Ice Sheet which projects into the Weddell Sea is in danger of disintegrating.[8] If this happened, it would raise sea levels by several metres. So, maybe *now* is the time we should start

5. Revelation 20:2,10
6. Genesis 3:22
7. Revelation 22:2 GNB
8. *The Independent*, 10 May 2012

listening to what God is telling us about being better servants of God's creation. Too often we allow ourselves to be lulled into inaction by the soothing mood music of modern capitalism. We are like the boy Mowgli in the Disney version of *The Jungle Book*, falling asleep among the coils of the snake as it sings "Trust in me." Meanwhile, the processes of *escalation* and *expulsion* that our ancestors unleashed into the world grow more and more powerful every day. Our population and demand for energy is escalating and large numbers of people are being expelled from their land because of flood, drought and war. *But* the Bible encourages us to believe that God still cares about us and our world; that Jesus, our Tree of Life, can still bring healing to the nations; and that it *is* possible, with God's help, to overcome the devious snake and live lives that bring blessing to our planet and to *all* its inhabitants—as Noah did; and as Adam and Eve were meant to do.

The Exhausted Land

Leviticus 25:1–13, 23

The Lord said to Moses at Mount Sinai, "Speak to the Israelites and say to them: 'When you enter the land I am going to give you, the land itself must observe a Sabbath to the Lord. For six years sow your fields, and for six years prune your vineyards and gather their crops. But in the seventh year the land is to have a year of Sabbath rest, a Sabbath to the Lord. Do not sow your fields or prune your vineyards. Do not reap what grows of itself or harvest the grapes of your untended vines. The land is to have a year of rest. Whatever the land yields during the Sabbath year will be food for you—for yourself, your male and female servants, and the hired worker and temporary resident who live among you, as well as for your livestock and the wild animals in your land. Whatever the land produces may be eaten."

"Count off seven Sabbath years—seven times seven years—so that the seven Sabbath years amount to a period of forty-nine years. Then have the trumpet sounded everywhere on the tenth day of the seventh month; on the Day of Atonement sound the trumpet throughout your land. Consecrate the fiftieth year and proclaim liberty throughout the land to all its inhabitants. It shall be a jubilee for you; each of you is to return to your family property and to your own clan. The fiftieth year shall be a jubilee for you; do not sow and do not reap what grows of itself or harvest the untended vines. For it is a jubilee and is to be holy for you; eat only what is taken directly from the fields. In this Year of Jubilee everyone is to return to their own property."

"The land must not be sold permanently, because the land is mine and you reside in my land as foreigners and strangers."

The Land of Canaan was to be for the Israelites what the Garden of Eden had been for Adam and Eve—a well-provisioned and beautiful environment. There, they had the opportunity to live in harmony with God, with each other, and with nature—so long as they remained humble and obedient. Just as the newly created couple had been warned about the need to observe limits on how much they took from their surroundings, so the newly created nation of Israel were warned about this too. It was all spelled out in the Law of Moses, and in the first seven verses of Leviticus 25, the Israelites are told to give the land they were farming one year off in every seven. The land was to enjoy its own Sabbath.

Back in Exodus 23:12, Moses had told the people, "six days do your work, but on the seventh day do not work, so that your ox and your donkey may rest and the slave born in your household, and the alien as well, may be refreshed." The Sabbath was one of God's limits, designed not just to prevent *people* from getting exhausted, but *animals* as well. This thought for animal welfare is consistent with God's love and care for all of his creation. The closing words of the Book of Jonah illustrate this perfectly because they record God asking the prophet why God wouldn't be concerned not just for the 120,000 inhabitants of Nineveh who were threatened with destruction but with the "many *cattle* as well."[1] God does not only pity the people, he pities their animals; he doesn't want *either* to suffer. So, as well as being instructed by Moses not to work their slaves into the ground, the Jews are instructed not to work their animals into the ground either. Their animal workers needed rest just as much as their human workers did.

However, Leviticus 25 extends this divine mandate even further. Not only are the animals to enjoy a Sabbath, but the land itself should enjoy one. In the case of the land, however, it was to be a Sabbath *year* rather than a Sabbath day. God says to his people in v4: "But in the seventh year

1. Jonah 4:11 (Italics added).

the land is to have a Sabbath of rest, a Sabbath to the Lord." The instruction is re-enforced in the following verse: "the land is to have a year of rest."

And that's not all! After this seven year cycle has been repeated seven times (i.e. after 49 years), the people were told to observe a kind of "*Super* Sabbath" when, not only was the land to be given an extra year off, but it was also to be returned to its original owners or their descendants. This fiftieth year was known as "The Year of Jubilee", or "The Year of Restoration," and the details of how the land should be both rested and re-distributed are described in vs. 8–28.

There are two key lessons we can draw from these instructions about the land that are relevant for us in the 21st century: *use it gently* and *hold it lightly*.

Use it gently

Telling the Jews to leave the land *fallow* on a regular basis made ecological sense because the continuous growing of the same crop year after year would drain the soil of particular nutrients. By giving the land a year to recover after six years of cultivation, the people would avoid the danger of the soil becoming exhausted and its productivity falling off. There is an intriguing parallel between the instructions about land in the first half of Leviticus chapter 25 and the instructions about slaves in the second half; each half ending with an almost identical summary (vs. 23 and 55). This is no coincidence because the land can very easily be treated as if it were a slave. The writer is therefore implying that God is just as opposed to the exploitation and abuse of the Israelites' land as he is to the exploitation and abuse of their human slaves. Like the slaves, the land needs to be given the opportunity to rest, and the chance to gain its freedom from assumed or unjust systems of ownership.

When we try to relate this teaching to today's world, however, we immediately face two difficulties. The first is our much greater levels of population. The number of human mouths that need feeding means that if land is left fallow for any length of time, people will starve. So, although it may not be wise to farm the same land continuously for risk of exhausting the soil, we have little option if we want to meet the growing need for food. The second difference from Bible times is the use of artificial fertilizers. Today, it is no longer necessary to leave land fallow for a year because farmers are able to add chemicals to the soil to replace the nutrients that have been lost through constant cultivation. The problem is that heavy use of artificial fertilizers brings its own dangers. It can lead to unhealthy levels of nitrogen and ammonia leaching into our water supply. It is also increasingly costly. Currently, five per cent of all natural gas used in the world goes into the production of ammonia for fertilizers[2]; and we all know what has been happening to gas prices!

Given these differences, it is clearly unrealistic in our modern, crowded world to expect that land can be given a Sabbath rest one year in every seven. But the general principle of not abusing land is still a good one. Land should not be seen simply as a resource to be exploited; it is our life-support system which needs careful handling. If we cultivate the soil too intensively, if we overdose it with too many chemicals, if we kill off too many of its natural bacteria, then it's *we* who will suffer. The land has been created and given by God for our use; but He wants us to use it gently.

There is a startling verse at the end of the book of 2 Chronicles. After describing how the King of Babylonia conquered Judah and carried off many of the inhabitants into exile, the writer makes this comment: "And so what the Lord had foretold through the prophet Jeremiah was fulfilled,

2. http://bit.ly/1clZtkN ("Fertilizers are chemical compounds used to pro-mote plant growth.")

'The land will lie desolate for seventy years, *to make up for the Sabbath rest that has not been observed'.*"[3] In other words, part of the reason for the exile—that terrible disaster that befell the Israelites—was their failure to allow their land a regular opportunity to rest and recover.

They exploited the land so much that, like an over-worked and harshly treated slave, it rose up against them and threw them out. This stands as a warning for our own generation. If we do not moderate the demands we make upon the land, it will rise up against us. Some areas of the world are already doing that. People are being forced into exile because their land has been so heavily cultivated, or its tree-cover so comprehensively cleared, that all the good soil has been blown or washed away. Even in Britain, the doubling of the number of houses that have paved over their front gardens to create car parking space between 1991 and 2011 has meant that heavy rain, instead of soaking into the ground, runs more quickly into drains and rivers to cause flooding.[4] It is therefore in all of our interests to treat land more gently. If that means the land doesn't produce as much as we want it to, then maybe that's OK. We in more prosperous countries need to be challenged to live more simply. Maybe it will cause us to trust more in the God who declares that: "Men and women shall not live by bread alone, but by every word that comes from the mouth of the Lord."[5]

3. 2 Chronicles 36:21 GNB (italics added).
4. *Spaced out: Perspectives on Parking Policy* RAC Foundation Report: quoted in ht tp://bit.ly/1clZvJt ("UK's front gardens paved over for parking spaces, report shows", *The Guardian*). See also http://bit.ly/1clZvJu. ("Death of the British front garden leaves cities in peril of flooding", *The Observer*, 15 August 2004)
5. Deuteronomy 8:3.

Hold it lightly

Ownership of land is a very important issue in developed countries today. In particular countries like the UK and the US a much higher proportion of people own their own homes even when compared to other European countries. As the saying goes, "An Englishman's home is his castle!" Leviticus 25 doesn't allow the Jews to think like that. They might wish they could build a big fence around their field to keep all its produce for themselves; but it wasn't allowed. During each harvest, the Israelites had to let the local poor onto their land so that they could follow workers and pick up any corn that was dropped. These poor people could also pick corn from the edges of the field. More than that; every seventh year farmers were required to withdraw their workers completely and let anyone come onto their field and pick what was growing naturally. During this Sabbath year, the produce of every field belonged to everyone. People could forage for food wherever they found it growing, just like they did during their wilderness wanderings. This "help yourself" invitation wasn't just for the human poor; it was also extended to local livestock and wild animals (v7). It is very difficult to feel *possessive* about one's land when, every seven years, it becomes everyone else's land too!

An even bigger shake-up happened every fifty years. *Then,* all land that had been bought and sold during the previous half century had to be handed back to its original owners (or to their descendants). This law stopped the territory assigned to each of the tribes from being broken up. It also prevented any one person from amassing huge amounts of property which they could then hand on to their descendants and so create an entrenched class system of rich land owners and poor peasants. This was an attempt to place a limit on the growth of inequalities. However much property someone acquired over the years, it all had to be handed back at the year of Jubilee.

In 2012 Britain celebrated its own kind of Jubilee, to mark the Queen's sixty years on the throne. Just imagine what would have happened had this followed the model of the Biblical Jubilee. Everyone, including the Royal Family, would have handed back all the land they had bought (or taken by force) from someone else. Everyone would have been released from their debts. All those working under conditions of virtual slavery would have been set free. Yes, it would be absolute chaos! But isn't there something rather attractive about the idea of re-distribution in these days of obscene inequality? Maybe the church should set an example by showing that some level of re-distribution is not just possible, but desirable. The first church did just that in Acts 4:

> There were no needy persons among them. For from time to time those who owned lands or houses sold them, brought the money from the sales, and put it at the apostles' feet, and it was distributed to anyone as they had need.[6]

Sadly, there is no evidence to suggest that the Jews in the Old Testament ever put the Jubilee Law into practice. There were huge inequalities by the time of Jesus, about which he was very critical. Thankfully, he was able to instil into his followers a new spirit of generosity so that the Early Church put in place its own version of the Jubilee. Maybe we need to recover something of that same spirit. Certainly, we should take to heart the words of v23 which insist that if we've got land or property, we must hold it lightly because it's not actually ours; it belongs to God. He allows us to make use of it not just for our own blessing, but for the blessing of others. We should therefore share the benefits of the land we've been given stewardship of; for example, by offering more hospitality, by opening up our gardens, by setting up

6. Acts 4:34–35

community orchards[7], by joining a "landshare" scheme[8], or by
engaging in some "guerrilla gardening" in areas of neglected
or unsightly public land.[9] Through actions like these, and by
treating it gently and by holding it lightly,

> The desert and the parched land will be glad;
>> the wilderness will rejoice and blossom.
> Like the crocus, it will burst into bloom;
>> it will rejoice greatly and shout for joy![10]

---

7. http://bit.ly/1clZOEa ("Community orchards: a 'how to' guide", UK Government)
8. http://www.landshare.org.uk/
9. http://www.farmgarden.org.uk/guerrilla-gardening
10. Isaiah 35:1-2

The Mighty Crocodile

Psalm 8:1–2, 6–8

O Lᴏʀᴅ, our Lord,
> how majestic is your name in all the earth!
You have set your glory above the heavens.
From the lips of children and infants
> you have ordained praise because of your enemies,
to silence the foe and the avenger. You made [humankind]
> ruler over the works of your hands
you put everything under their feet:
> all flocks and herds, and the beasts of the field,
> the birds of the air, and the fish of the sea.

Job 42:1–6; 12–17

Then Job replied to the Lᴏʀᴅ:

> "I know that you can do all things;
> > no purpose of yours can be thwarted.
> You asked, 'Who is this that obscures my plans without
> > knowledge?'
> > Surely I spoke of things I did not understand,
> > things too wonderful for me to know.

> "You said, 'Listen now, and I will speak;
> > I will question you,

and you shall answer me.'
My ears had heard of you
but now my eyes have seen you.
Therefore I despise myself
and repent in dust and ashes."

…

The LORD blessed the latter part of Job's life more than the former part. He had fourteen thousand sheep, six thousand camels, a thousand yoke of oxen and a thousand donkeys. And he also had seven sons and three daughters. The first daughter he named Jemimah, the second Keziah and the third Keren-Happuch. Nowhere in all the land were there found women as beautiful as Job's daughters, and their father granted them an inheritance along with their brothers.

After this, Job lived a hundred and forty years; he saw his children and their children to the fourth generation. And so Job died, an old man and full of years.

As Kingfishers Catch Fire

As kingfishers catch fire, dragonflies draw flame;
As tumbled over rim in roundy wells
Stones ring; like each tucked string tells, each hung bell's
Bow swung finds tongue to fling out broad its name;
Each mortal thing does one thing and the same:
Deals out that being indoors each one dwells;
Selves—goes itself; *myself* it speaks and spells,
Crying *What I do is me: for that I came*.

I say more: the just man justices;
Keeps grace: that keeps all his goings graces;
Acts in God's eye what in God's eye he is—
Christ—for Christ plays in ten thousand places,
Lovely in limbs, and lovely in eyes not his
To the Father through the features of men's faces.

Gerard Manley Hopkins[1]

1. *The poems of Gerard Manley Hopkins*, Oxford: Oxford University Press, 1967.

Most of the Book of Job is taken up with a very emotional dialogue between Job and his friends about why God allows suffering. Job doesn't feel he deserves all the terrible things that have happened to him, whilst his friends maintain that he must have, because God is always just and would never punish the innocent. The arguments go to and fro until we reach chapter 38, where the opening words "Then the Lord answered Job out of the storm" raise our hopes that we will finally get an answer to this thorny issue of suffering.

But instead of answering Job's complaints, God spends the next four chapters waxing lyrical about the wonders of Creation and challenging Job to admit that none of these wonders are any of Job's doing. "Were you there when I laid the earth's foundation?" God asks in chapter 38. "Have you journeyed to the springs of the sea? Do you send lightning bolts on their way?"[2] In chapter 39, God moves on to the wild animals and asks Job how much he knows about them, and then in chapters 40 and 41, focuses on two particularly impressive examples. Firstly, he describes the monster Behemoth (probably the hippopotamus or elephant) which he says, "ranks first among the works of God."[3] Then he spends the whole of chapter 41 marvelling over Leviathan which, although sometimes used in scripture to represent the primeval force of watery chaos, is here almost certainly meant to signify the crocodile. This is how the chapter ends: "Nothing on earth is his equal—a creature without fear. He looks down on all that are haughty; he is king over all that are proud."[4]

It's a great climax to a fascinating four chapters, but we are still left wondering: What's all this got to do with Job's troubles? Why does God choose to respond to Job's question about human suffering by giving him a lecture on ecology and zoology? Maybe God wants Job to realize that there's no point in trying to understand why suffering exists in the world until

2. Job 38:4,16,35
3. Job 40:19
4. Job 41:33–34

we have begun to understand why the world itself exists in the first place. In other words, before we ask "Why suffering?" we should first ask "Why the world?... Why the crocodile?"

This question is crucial because there is a great temptation for us to think and act as though this world was made purely for the use and enjoyment of human beings. We refer to water, coal, copper, and so on, as "natural resources"—as if to be a resource for our use is the only reason they exist. We cram animals and birds into sheds and battery farms so that we can make as much profit out of their meat and eggs as possible. We don't concern ourselves too much with the quality of their lives because surely the sole purpose of their existence is to provide us with food and finance. We take it for granted that *our* needs and desires will always take precedence over every other consideration. And certainly we can find some support for this attitude in the pages of the Bible. In Genesis 1, God gave men and women dominion over all of creation (v26). In Psalm 8, the poet says to God, "You made [mankind] ruler over the works of your hands, you put everything under his feet; all flocks and herds, and the beasts of the field, the birds of the air, and the fish of the sea" (v6–8). Passages like these can encourage us to assume that all created things exist for our benefit.

However, if we do assume this, then the existence within that world of something that *doesn't* benefit us—like suffering—becomes a real problem. It seems to go against the very reason why the world was created. But what if simply to meet the needs and desires of human beings *wasn't* the reason the world was created?

Imagine we have been invited to a friend's birthday party and decide to be really helpful by taking round a plate of cheese and pickle sandwiches. Suppose one of the other guests responds to the proffered plate by saying "I can't eat those—they've got pickle in! Why has she gone and ruined a perfectly good cheese sandwich by adding that horrible stuff? I'd never use pickle if it was *my* party!" We would probably reply,

"But this *isn't* your party; it's *her* party, and if *she* wants to make a plate-full of cheese and pickle sandwiches, she's perfectly entitled to do so!" And we would be right. The point is that although we have been invited to enjoy the party, including the food, the party isn't primarily *for us*. The same could be said about Creation. God has invited us to enjoy the world, including the food (and the many other things) it provides; but that doesn't mean the world was created *for us*. It doesn't mean that it's *our* Creation and we can treat it however we like. It's not *our* party.

The Apostle Paul is quite clear who the universe is for—it's for Jesus. He says in Colossians 1:16 "God created the whole universe through him *and for him*." In Ephesians 1:10, he tells us that God's plan is "to bring all creation together, everything in heaven and on earth, *with Christ as head*." In other words, Creation exists first and foremost to give pleasure to the Son, just as it originally gave pleasure to the Father as he viewed the newly created universe and declared it good.[5] We get a glimpse of that pleasure in chapters 38–41 of Job where we hear God revelling in the way the stars appear to sing together,[6] the way the wild deer gives birth,[7] the way the ostrich is so clumsy and yet so fast,[8] the way the hippopotamus hides among the reeds in the swamp,[9] and so on. This appreciation of each feature of creation simply for being what it is underpins Gerard Manley Hopkins' poem *As Kingfishers catch fire*. Whether it's the sight of a kingfisher or a dragonfly; whether it's the sound of a tumbling stone or a swinging bell;

> Each mortal thing does one thing and the same:
>> deals out that being indoors each one dwells;
> Selves—goes itself...

5. Genesis 1:31
6. Job 38:7
7. Job 39:1–4
8. Job 39:13–18
9. Job 40:21

God derives great pleasure from watching each part of his creation being itself; displaying those unique qualities that make it what it is. The object of God's admiration doesn't have to be useful; it doesn't even have to be attractive; it simply has to be itself.

We get a hint of this in Psalm 8 where it says, "From the lips of children and infants you have ordained praise" (v2). How do infants praise God? They are too young to have any concept of the divine; their language skills (if they have any at all) are very limited. Their praise must take the form of simply being themselves—gurgling and crying, discovering their own fingers, reaching out to the hazy world around them. The chief priests and teachers of the law in Matthew 21 didn't understand this, which is why they got so annoyed with the children shouting "Hosanna to the Son of David!" in the temple.[10]

For them the sound of some lively children shouting things they couldn't possibly understand wasn't honouring to God. Jesus responded by quoting Psalm 8:2 and rejoicing in the fact that these children felt able to express the excitement, enthusiasm, and responsiveness that their Creator had endowed them with.

As well as illustrating the delight God took in his creation, God's speech to Job in chapters 38–41 has the effect of puncturing humanity's over-inflated view of itself. It balances out those scriptures that speak of how important men and women are in the purposes of God. It's as if God is saying: "Yes, you humans *are* important; but *not* as important as you seem to think! Because you believe you come first among all my works, *I'm* giving that title to the hippo! (40:19); and because you proudly assume you can rule over all living things, let me remind you that the crocodile, 'is king over all that are proud!'" (41:34). God takes the trouble, when describing the great strength of the crocodile, to use language that belittles human technology. Our fish-hooks, ropes, harpoons, spears,

10. Matthew 21:15–16

swords, arrows and clubs are all useless at controlling him;[11] his back is like "a row of shields" (v15), and "iron he treats like straw and bronze like rotten wood" (v27). In other words, human beings must not consider themselves to be the be-all-and-end-all of God's Creation. God's speech to Job is designed to change this *human*-centred view of the world and replace it with a *God*-centred view. Human beings may have been called to rule over all living things, but only on *Christ's* behalf, in *his* image, and for the benefit of *his* creation.

In his painting *The Scorpion* (Figure 3 on the following page) Stanley Spencer offers us a thoughtful image of what this might mean. The picture forms part of Spencer's *Christ in the Wilderness* series and shows Jesus sitting on the desert floor during his forty days of temptation. The feet bare to the stony ground and the hands open to the scorpion suggest a man who is in touch with nature; while the similarity between the shape and colour of his skin and clothing and that of the surrounding landscape and sky makes him look like he is at home in the natural world. The scene lends support to the statement in Mark 1:13 that Jesus "was *with* the wild animals;" a statement that conveys a sense of companionship.

Even though the scorpion in Spencer's painting has its tail curled over and sting ready, Jesus continues to let it rest on his open hand, looking as if he empathises with the animal's vulnerability. Maybe he can still hear the scripture that Satan had tempted him with: "He will command his angels concerning you, and they will lift you up in their hands."[12] As he lifts the scorpion up in *his* hands, it's as if Jesus is symbolising his mission to lift up all of the earth and its inhabitants so that they can become what God created them to be; so that they can, as Hopkins says, "deal out that being indoors each one dwells." If we are to do the same it will involve respecting nature's wildness. We may prefer a

11. Job 41:1,7,26,29
12. Matthew 4:6

Figure 3: Stanley Spencer—*The Scorpion*.

scorpion without a sting, but that's not how God made it. All the animals described in Job chapters 38–41 are essentially *wild* (with the exception of the war horse, which can hardly be called domesticated!). The independence of spirit displayed by these animals clearly gives God great satisfaction and therefore it should please us too.

Barry Richardson argues that we need to engage with the wildness of creation for our own health and well-being. Without contact with forces and creatures that challenge us, we lose touch with who we really are. Richardson goes on to give the following illustration:

> Let us imagine a 'conversation' with a wolf in its natural environment, accidentally met on a forest path, and a second 'conversation', this time with our family dog in a local park. The wolf is... essentially other as it stands and looks at us and its assessment of us is in its own terms, not ours. ...It seems to ask, 'Stranger, interloper, what role do you play in the forest? What is your reaction to me? What do I do about your presence here?'
>
> Our dog, on the other hand, has been bred and trained to say what we want to hear: 'I like being with you. You are never wrong. You are wonderful'.[13]

In other words, a natural world that is increasingly controlled and domesticated by human activity is not good for our psychological welfare. It encourages delusions of our independence from the rest of creation and restricts the opportunities for self-discovery that come from interacting with creatures that challenge us with their "other-ness".

13. *Use, Preserve, Enable? A Moral Basis for Environmental Management Decisions, and its Consequences*, Ecotheology, 8(2), December 2003, p196

As well as the wild animals, God tells Job that he revels in the wild power of the sea and the weather. He even speaks to Job out of the storm.[14] We don't particularly like storms. Along with other unpredictable weather events, they can disrupt our lives and sometimes cause suffering and death. But these natural processes, which can border on the chaotic, are all part of the freedom that God grants to his Creation. He didn't create the world to be a machine whose workings were rigid and predictable; he created it to be a home for millions of living things, each with the freedom to be, to grow, to interact and to evolve. The resulting planet, composed of moving tectonic plates, dynamic weather, and living plants and animals, produces order *and* chaos, pleasure *and* pain, growth *and* decay, life *and* death. According to the scientist James Lovelock, the earth itself behaves a bit like a self-regulating organism, which he has named Gaia. We often refer to the rainforests as the "lungs of the earth", as if we too see the earth as a living body that breathes in carbon dioxide and breathes out oxygen—just like we do (only the other way round!).

All of this means that God has an interest and concern for the earth that is *independent* of his concern for us. He loves it and appreciates it for its own sake and not just for its usefulness to human beings. God says to Job, "Who makes rain fall where no one lives? Who waters the dry and thirsty land so that grass springs up?"[15] The answer of course is God, and he does it simply for the benefit of the land and the vegetation, not (in this case) for the benefit of any human beings. If we accept that God created the earth through the long process of evolution, then to hold an arrogant human-centred view makes no sense at all, since God will have enjoyed a relationship with the earth and its many different life-forms for millions of years before we humans ever arrived on the scene.

None of this is to say that human beings aren't special; or that we aren't unique in our level of understanding and ability

14. Job 38:1; 40:6
15. Job 38:26–27 GNB

to respond to our Creator. We have indeed been given the incredible privilege of being God's representatives on earth, exercising his rule over all other living things. But, as we've seen in earlier chapters, such rule is to be exercised *in the image of God* who allows and enables each part of Creation to glorify God in its own way.

After hearing God describe the wonder and wildness of the earth and its animals, Job begins to see his own situation from a different perspective. His response is to say, "Surely I spoke of things I did not understand, things too wonderful for me to know...Therefore I despise myself and repent in dust and ashes" (42:3,6). The Hebrew in v6 is a bit obscure and the use of the word "repent" seems a bit strong given that the whole point of the Book of Job is to show that his sufferings *weren't* a punishment for sin. A better translation of that verse may be: "I am ashamed [of all I have said] and realize that I am dust and ashes". Job realised that, like Adam, he was made of the same dust as all the animals he had just heard God praise. So, who was *he* to demand a hearing from God? Who was *he* to insist on his rights? Any special relationship that he might have with his creator depended solely on God's *grace*, not on any privileged position he might occupy at the top of some animal hierarchy.

The happy ending described in the final chapter of Job can seem far too neat and heartless. How can the gift of ten new children make up for the terrible loss of the ten Job had before? And yet, looking at it from an ecological perspective, the message contained in the book's conclusion is stunning. It shows that God's speech had indeed made a profound difference to the way Job viewed the world.[16] After being informed that Job fathered seven new sons and three new daughters, the author then tells us the names of his three daughters: Jemimah, Keziah and Keren Happuch. Not the names of the sons, notice—just the names of the

---

16. I am indebted to Norman Wirzba's *The Paradise of God*, Oxford: OUP, 2003, p.47 for drawing my attention to the importance of Job's daughters.

daughters. This is very unusual in such a male-dominated society. But, even more radical than that, we're told that Job, "granted them an inheritance along with their brothers" (v15). Such equal treatment was revolutionary. Finally, we are told that, "nowhere in all the land were there women as beautiful as Job's daughters" (v15).

So, here is a man who gives names to those works of God's creation that are normally overlooked as being of less value, who affirms his daughters' uniqueness and allows them, in the words of Hopkins, to "fling out broad [their] name," to act, "...in God's eye what in God's eye [they are]". Here is a man who no longer thinks in terms of hierarchies, but who gives to all his children according to his loving grace. And here is a man who appreciates the beauty of God's handiwork as it is displayed in the appearance and personalities of his daughters, and no doubt also in the appearance and individuality of the many other creatures God has helped him to see with fresh eyes. Job no longer has a *human*-centred view of the world; he now has gained a *God*-centred view; and although there are still many things he doesn't understand, at least he is looking at them through better spectacles!

The question of why God allows suffering still remains. The Book of Job gives us permission to keep asking it whilst at the same time alerting us to the limits of our understanding. It reminds us that wildness, mystery and unpredictability are intrinsic to the planet on which we live; and that our sufferings will only be made worse by a refusal to accept this. Our relentless efforts to domesticate and exploit the natural world purely for our own ends risk creating even more chaotic and unpredictable side-effects. Maybe there's more wisdom than we realize in God's warning about the crocodile. "Can you fill his hide with harpoons or his head with fishing spears?" he asks Job. "If you lay a hand on him, you will remember the struggle and never do it again!"[17]

17. Job 41:7–8

The crocodile—like many other things in our world—may be dangerous, but we should see this as a reminder and a challenge from God to treasure our planet for all the strange and amazing life-forms it supports, and to follow the One who was content to be "*with* the wild animals".

The Sacred Oak

Psalm 24:1–7

The earth is the Lord's, and everything in it,
    the world, and all who live in it;
for he founded it on the seas
    and established it on the waters.

Who may ascend the mountain of the Lord?
    Who may stand in his holy place?
The one who has clean hands and a pure heart,
    who does not trust in an idol
    or swear by what is false.

They will receive blessing from the Lord
    and vindication from God their Saviour.
Such is the generation of those who seek him,
    who seek your face, God of Jacob.

Lift up your heads, you gates;
    be lifted up, you ancient doors,
    that the King of glory may come in.

Genesis 12:6–7

Abram travelled through the land [of Canaan] as far as the site of the great tree of Moreh at Shechem. At that time the Canaanites were in the land. The Lord appeared to Abram and said, "To your offspring I will give this land." So he built an altar there to the Lord, who had appeared to him.

Many scholars think that Psalm 24 was written to celebrate or commemorate the occasion when the Ark of God—the elaborate box containing the tablets of the Law—was carried into Jerusalem, and later into the temple. We read in 1 Chronicles 16 that there was much singing when David brought the ark into his newly conquered capital city; and in 2 Chronicles 5 that there was even more singing when his son Solomon had it processed into the newly built temple. The ark represented the divine presence, so when it was finally carried into the Temple, it was as if God himself was arriving in person. Hence the refrain: "Lift up your heads, O you gates; be lifted up, you ancient doors, that the King of glory may come in" (vs7, 9). However, it is also possible to read this psalm from an ecological perspective, and see the temple as representing not just a building but the whole of God's creation.

The psalm begins with the assertion: "The earth is the Lord's, and everything in it, the world and all who live in it; for he founded it upon the seas and established it upon the waters." These words refer back to Genesis 1 when God created land out of the chaotic waters. The language makes it sound as if God was erecting *a building*. The same construction language is used in other scriptures. For example, in Job 38 God says, "On what were [the earth's] footings set, or who laid its cornerstone?" (v6); and in Isaiah 48, he says, "My own hand laid the foundations of the earth" (v13). The impression given by such references to footings, cornerstones and foundations is that God was building some kind of temple for the display of his glory, and that temple was the earth itself. So maybe, when the psalmist calls out for the gates to be flung wide and the ancient doors to be opened, he could be referring not to God's entry into the temple in Jerusalem, but to his entry into the temple of the natural world.

There are, of course, many biblical examples of people encountering the presence of God within nature long before there was any designated tent or building. When Abram first arrived in the land of Canaan, he built an altar next to "the great tree of Moreh" (Genesis 12:6) because it was through that oak tree that the Lord appeared to him (v7). Maybe this old tree was already a sacred place for local people. Maybe it exuded a sense of permanence and strength that was reassuring to a traveller who felt insecure in an unknown land, and its branches resembled giant arms opening wide to offer him welcome and protection. Either way, we're told that God appeared to Abram through the majesty of that oak tree.

Abram's experience is beautifully captured by the German romantic artist Casper David Friedrich in his painting *Winter Landscape with Church* (Figure 4 on the next page)[1]. Looked at carefully, it is possible to make out a man leaning against the right side of the rock in the centre of the picture. He is gazing up at a wooden crucifix that has been erected in front of a large fir tree. Like Abraham, this traveller has arrived at a holy tree where someone has built the equivalent of an altar. Lying on the snow are two crutches which the man has thrown down, either in ecstasy or exhaustion. In the background, we can make out the silhouette of a Gothic church, shimmering in the mist. We wonder whether it was to this church that the pilgrim was heading. Is this tree just a stop along the way or has he encountered the divine presence right here

1. I am indebted to the helpful analysis of this painting in Joseph Leo Koerner, *Casper David Friedrich and the Subject of Landscape*, London: Reaktion, 2009, pp. 23-28.

Figure 4: Casper David Friedrich—*Winter Landscape with Church.*

beneath its branches? Surely it is significant that the fir grove mirrors the shape of the church. Is Friedrich telling us that the trees too form a house of God? Certainly, it is the trees and not the church that take centre stage, with the tallest one rising to the same height as the building's pinnacles. We then notice that the second tallest tree actually blocks the traveller's view of the church. Maybe he doesn't even realize the church is there. Once we begin to focus on this second, rather unremarkable tree, we perceive that it lies at the very centre of the picture flanked on one side by the church and on the other by the crucifix. Maybe we are being encouraged to see that the tree can be just as much a place of encounter with the divine as the church and the crucifix. In fact, being an evergreen in the depths of winter makes this tree uniquely able to communicate the everlasting love of God to those whose lives feel as bleak as this landscape.

Sadly, in later centuries, the descendants of Abraham lost sight of God's presence in nature and focused more and more on man-made temples. Isaiah criticised them for this with words that were later quoted by the martyr Stephen:

> The Most High does not live in houses built by men; as the prophet says, 'Heaven is my throne, and the earth is my footstool. What kind of house would you build for me, says the Lord? Or where will my resting place be? Has not my hand made all these things?[2]

Somehow the Jews had forgotten that the covenant box, housed within their elaborate temple, contained stone tablets that were originally dug from a mountainside, chiselled in the open air and carried for forty years through a desert. As such, it represented a God whose presence was first experienced *outside*, within the temple of his created universe. And this experience wasn't unusual. The list of Biblical

2. Isaiah 66:1-2; Acts 7:48-50

characters who encountered God in or through Nature is a long one, and includes[3]:

- Adam and Eve hearing God walk by in a garden.

- Noah hearing God's promise as he gazed up at a rainbow.

- Abraham hearing God speak through a tree, and later while gazing up at the night sky.

- Jacob discovering God in the middle of a desert, and while wading through a river.

- Moses, hearing God's call through a burning bush.

- The Israelites seeing God's glory within Mount Sinai's volcanic fire and smoke.

- Balaam receiving divine guidance through a donkey.

- Elijah miraculously fed by ravens.

- Elisha's servant seeing heavenly chariots of fire on hills gilded red by the rising sun,

- Job hearing God speak from a whirlwind.

- Ezekiel having a vision of God within an approaching desert storm.

- Jesus meeting with God on his early morning hill-walks.

- The disciples encountering the divine in the middle of a lake-storm.

- Peter, James and John hearing God speak from mountain-top clouds.

- Mary Magdalene meeting the risen Christ's among the trees and flowers of a garden.

---

3. Genesis 3:8; Genesis 9:12-17; Genesis 12:6-7 and 15:5; Genesis 28:10-16; Genesis 32:22-30; Exodus 3:1-6; Exodus 24:17; 1 Kings 17:1-6; 2 Kings 6:17; Job 38:1; Ezekiel 1:4-28; Mark 1:35; Mark 4:35-41; Mark 9:2-7; John 20:15-16.

In each of these examples, Nature is acting as a kind of *sacrament*. This term is normally applied to the bread and wine of the Eucharist and to the waters of baptism because it expresses how the ordinary elements of bread, wine and water can become the conveyors of deeper spiritual blessing. How this actually happens is a mystery; we just know from experience that through these things we receive God's grace.

Many people would say the same about their experience of other elements of nature. The theologian Rosemary Radford Ruether accommodates this by identifying two broad Christian responses to the natural world which she terms the *Covenantal* and the *Sacramental*.[4] By *Covenantal*, she means the approach that draws heavily on the legal basis for environmental care that is found in the Bible. It has formed the basis of much of this book's argument so far. We have looked at Adam and Eve's obligations to be good stewards and servants of Creation; we have noted the consequences of their failure to meet these obligations; we have seen how the Jews were instructed to give the land a Sabbath rest one year in every seven; and so on. Such an emphasis on legal requirements not only sits comfortably within the Protestant tradition, but it also lies behind many international treaties that seek to limit global warming and preserve bio-diversity. The trouble is that it has a tendency to become rather dry and soul-less. The Covenantal response needs to be complemented by something that stresses the emotional and spiritual aspects of humanity's interactions with nature.

That is why Ruether argues for an equal emphasis to be given to the Sacramental, a dimension that is more commonly associated with the Catholic tradition and which also draws on contributions from other religions. Previous chapters have touched on the sacramental by including two evocative poems by the Catholic priest Gerard Manley Hopkins; but it needs to be explored in more detail.

4. "Ecology and Theology: Ecojustice at the Center of the Church's Mission", *Interpretation*, 65(4), October 2011, pp. 354-363.

A Sacramental Approach to Nature

To treat the natural world as a sacrament means that it's not enough to know in our heads the obligations that God gives us towards his Creation; we must also experience in our hearts the nourishment that God gives us through his Creation. This is important firstly, to enrich our spiritual relationship with God, and secondly, to motivate our righteous behaviour towards the earth.

1. A sacramental approach enriches spirituality.

We do not care for Nature simply because God tells us to, but because Nature is a means through which God speaks to us and blesses us. The earth is not just a stage on which to obey God; it's also a venue in which to *meet* God—in many different ways; and by damaging that venue, we risk reducing the number and quality of the encounters available to us. As Edward P. Echlin noted, when lamenting the rate of human-caused species extinction, "God will never again communicate with men through a passenger pigeon or a dwarf caribou. Men can make extinct the voices of God."[5]

A sacramental approach helps us to be open to and to treasure the variety of spiritual experience that our natural world makes possible. This was the great legacy of the Romantic Movement that began in the late eighteenth century as a reaction to the way scientific discoveries seemed to reduce Nature to little more than an amalgam of physical laws and mechanical forces. Through their magical scenes, artists like Casper David Friedrich, William Blake and Samuel Palmer wanted to recover a natural world that didn't exist merely to be measured and examined, but to be *seen and felt*. The same was true for the Romantic poets, as we can see in the following extract from William Wordsworth's *Lines written a few miles above Tintern Abbey*:

5. Echlin, *Earth Spirituality*, New Alresford: Arthur James/John Hunt Publishing, 1999, p. 113.

My dear, dear Sister! and this prayer I make
Knowing that Nature never did betray
The heart that loved her; 'tis her privilege
Through all the years of this our life, to lead
From joy to joy: for she can so inform
The mind that is within us, so impress
With quietness and beauty, and so feed
With lofty thoughts, that neither evil tongues
Rash judgments, nor the sneers of selfish men
... Shall e'er prevail against us, or disturb
Our cheerful faith that all which we behold
Is full of blessings.[6]

Just as the Romantic Movement was necessary to add a sense of wonder to the bare scientific facts of the Enlightenment; so the Sacramental approach is necessary to do the same for the bare environmental laws of the Bible. The extra dimension it offers was well expressed by the Jewish scholar Martin Buber in his 1923 book called *I and Thou*.[7] Buber's thesis was that often we treat other people and other objects as if they were an "it"—something we view, measure and use for our own purposes. They remain detached from us and at our disposal. Most of the time, such an approach may be necessary in order to cope with the rush and bustle of life. But, says Buber, from time to time there need to be moments when this "I-It" relationship becomes an "I-Thou" one; when the person or landscape we encounter fills our senses and at that moment becomes everything; when they not only give themselves to us but call us to give ourselves to them. For a few magical minutes we find ourselves marvelling at the uniqueness and wonder of a flower or a sunset or a loved one.

Someone who expresses these I-Thou moments beautifully is Annie Dillard. In her book "Pilgrim at Tinker Creek," she describes being transfixed by the sight of a glowing cedar tree.

6. From *Lyrical Ballads,* William Wordsworth.
7. Martin Buber, *I and Thou*, New York: Scribner, 2000.

It was less like seeing than like being for the first time seen, knocked breathless by a powerful glance. The flood of fire abated, but I'm still spending the power. Gradually the lights went out in the cedar, the colors died, the cells unflamed and disappeared. I was still ringing. I had been my whole life a bell and never knew it until at that moment I was lifted and struck.[8]

Dillard also quotes the words of another author, Stephen Graham:

As you sit on the hillside, or lie prone under the trees of the forest, or sprawl wet-legged on the shingly beach of a mountain stream, the great door, that does not look like a door, opens.[9]

For Dillard, this mysterious door opens to reveal both the uniqueness of that particular moment *and* the presence of the divine in that moment. The image of an opening door takes us back to Psalm 24: "Fling wide the gates, open the ancient doors, and the great king will come in."[10] We suddenly discover, as Jacob did, that "Surely the Lord is in this place, and I was not aware of it."[11] Such precious experiences, even though they don't last very long, not only enrich our sense of God presence; they also help to motivate us to action.

2. A sacramental approach motivates behaviour.

Sometimes mere knowledge of the facts is insufficient to galvanise action. Moses knew all about the sufferings of his

---

8. Dillard, *Pilgrim at Tinker Creek*, Norwich: Canterbury Press, 2011, p. 36.
9. Ibid, p. 81
10. Psalm 24:7 GNB
11. Genesis 28:16

people in Egypt but would have stayed minding sheep in Midian had he not encountered God in the burning bush. Balaam was fully aware that cursing the Israelites was forbidden but he would have cursed them all the same had he not heard God's voice speaking through his donkey. In the same way, it doesn't seem to be enough for us simply to *know* the Biblical injunctions about caring for God's creation or the facts about the damage being done to the environment.

Only a personal revelation of God's sacramental presence in nature can make this knowledge effective in changing our lifestyles. We see this happening to the main character in Barbara Kingsolver's climate change novel *Flight Behaviour.* Dellarobia Turnbow was on the way up a forest road to do something that would ruin her life when she is stopped short.

> A small shift between cloud and sun altered the daylight, and the whole landscape intensified, brightening before her eyes. The forest blazed with its own internal flame... The flame now appeared to lift from individual treetops in showers of orange sparks, exploding the way a pine log does in a campfire when it's poked...She was on her own here, staring at glowing trees. ...She couldn't remember when she'd had such room for being. This was not just another fake thing in her life's cheap chain of events, leading up to this day of sneaking around in someone else's thrown-away boots. Here that ended. Unearthly beauty had appeared to her, a vision of glory to stop her in the road.[12]

The novel goes on to show how this experience of seeing millions of butterflies profoundly affected the way she lived her life. None of us can manufacture moments like this; they

12. Kingsolver, *Flight Behaviour*, London: Faber and Faber, 2012, pp. 13-15.

are gifts from God. But we are more likely to receive them if we consider the whole of Creation to be God's temple and look for signs of his presence there; just as Abram did when he entered the land of Canaan and saw the great oak tree at Moreh. The attitude we should try to cultivate is perfectly captured by R. S. Thomas' poem *The Moor*:

> It was like a church to me.
> I entered it on soft foot,
> Breath held like a cap in the hand.
> It was quiet.
> What God was there made himself felt,
> Not listened to, in clean colours
> That brought a moistening of the eye,
> In movement of the wind over grass.
>
> There were no prayers said. But stillness
> Of the heart's passions—-that was praise
> Enough; and the mind's cession
> Of its kingdom. I walked on,
> Simple and poor, while the air crumbled
> And broke on me generously as bread.[13]

13. R S Thomas, *Collected Poems 1945-1990*, London: Phoenix, 1995, p. 166.

The Bumper Crop

Luke 12:13–21

Someone in the crowd said to him, "Teacher, tell my brother to divide the inheritance with me."

Jesus replied, "Man, who appointed me a judge or an arbiter between you?" Then he said to them, "Watch out! Be on your guard against all kinds of greed; life does not consist in an abundance of possessions."

And he told them this parable: "The ground of a certain rich man yielded an abundant harvest. He thought to himself, 'What shall I do? I have no place to store my crops'.

Then he said, 'This is what I'll do. I will tear down my barns and build bigger ones, and there I will store my surplus grain. And I'll say to myself, "You have plenty of grain laid up for many years. Take life easy; eat, drink and be merry."'

But God said to him, 'You fool! This very night your life will be demanded from you. Then who will get what you have prepared for yourself?' This is how it will be with whoever stores up things for themselves but is not rich toward God."

Luke 5:37–38

And no-one pours new wine into old wineskins. If he does, the new wine will run out and the wineskins will be ruined. No, new wine must be poured into new wineskins. And no-one after drinking the old wine wants the new, for he says, 'The old is better.'

A Short Sketch

Scene: a well-dressed couple are sitting reading menus at a table in a posh restaurant. A waiter approaches.

Waiter: Are you ready to order?

Lady: There are so many wonderful meals here; I don't know what to have.

Man (*to waiter*): Is there one you would recommend?

Waiter: The duck is particularly good today, sir.

Lady (*reading*): "Duck in lemon sauce." Yes, that *does* sound good. I'll have it.

Man: And I'll have the same.

Waiter: Certainly. Anything to drink, Sir?

Man: Have you got champagne?

Waiter: Of course.

Man: What's the best you've got?

Waiter: We have one bottle here which is vintage 1812. I believe the grapes were trodden by Napoleon himself.

Man: How much is it?

Waiter: £2000.

Man: We'll have it.

Lady: Oh, darling!

Waiter: Certainly, sir. I will go and fetch it from our cellar right away.

Lady: Oh, before you go; could you get me another wine glass, please.

Waiter: Is Madam not happy with her wine glass?

Lady: No, I'm not. For one thing, it's filthy dirty.

Waiter: My apologies, Madam. (*gets out hanky and wipes it*)

Man (*shocked*): What are you doing?

Waiter: I'm cleaning Madam's wine glass.

Lady: But you used your own hanky!

Waiter: Madam is very observant.

Lady: But you might have used that hanky to blow your nose.

Waiter: I believe I have, madam. I've been suffering with a bad cold all day and it's gone to my nose. Unfortunately, noses like mine run in the family.

Lady: And now it's run in my wine glass! I'm sorry, but I am not drinking from a glass that has been smeared with the contents of your nose. In any case, the glass has a crack in it.

Waiter: Is madam not happy with the crack?

Man: Not happy? Of course, she's not happy! If you fill that glass with wine, it will drip out of the crack onto the tablecloth.

Waiter: Sir is right (*pause*) I will go and get a saucer to put under the glass; it will catch the drips.

Lady: But I don't want a saucer; I want a new wine glass!

Waiter: Perhaps I could get the crack sealed for you.

Man: What?

Waiter: I notice that Mr Goldstein is sitting at table 6. I believe he is the manager of a glass blowing factory. I could ask him to come over.

Lady: But what can *he* do?

Waiter: Well, I imagine that he could put some special sealant along the crack to make it water-tight; or perhaps I should say "wine-tight."

Lady: But I will still be able to see where the crack was.

Waiter: Not if I blow out your candle and dim the lights.

Man: Let me get this right. I am buying the most expensive bottle of wine in your restaurant—for £2000—and you are expecting my wife to pour it into a dirty, cracked wine glass?

Waiter: Oh no, sir (*pause*) *I'll* pour it for her.

Man: I don't care *who* pours it! A bottle of vintage champagne deserves a new wine glass, and if you don't bring us a new glass right now, we will leave.

Waiter: I'm sorry (*turning to lady*) Madam, I will fetch you a new wine glass immediately.

(*picks up glass*).

Lady: Thank you. This whole episode has been so upsetting (*sniff*) it's brought tears to my eyes.

Waiter: (*takes out hanky & offers*) Use this, Madam. (*couple look horrified and freeze*)

It's clear that the human race is using up natural resources faster than the earth can replace them. It takes Mother Nature a lot longer to grow a tree than it does for us to chop it down for paper; and a lot longer still to produce a litre of oil than it does for us to extract it for use in our cars. The demand for timber, oil and other resources will only increase as world population grows and as those in developing countries aspire to the same affluent lifestyles we enjoy in the West. If we accept that the earth cannot go on providing what our current lifestyle demands of it; maybe it's time we took a long, hard look at our lifestyle.

In Luke 12, we're told that, "someone in the crowd said to [Jesus], 'Teacher, tell my brother to divide the inheritance with me'" (v13). Jesus' response was rather abrupt: "Man, who appointed me a judge or an arbiter between you?" Such abruptness isn't typical of Jesus, so it begs the question as to why he acted like this here. Maybe it was because Jesus sensed danger—the danger of being sucked in to the lifestyle assumptions of the surrounding culture. The phrase "Someone in the crowd" may be more than just a banal introduction; it may indicate that this man was among others sympathetic to his cause; that the crowd weren't just around him, they were *behind* him in the sense of supporting him. One can imagine him moaning about how unfairly he'd been treated, and being encouraged by the other members of the crowd to raise the matter with Jesus.

He squeezes through to the front and catches Jesus' eye, confident in the belief that everyone thought he was in the right. Maybe that's why, instead of humbly asking Jesus for help, the man issues Jesus with an order: "Teacher, *tell* my brother to divide the inheritance with me." Is it arrogance that made this man think he could simply command Jesus like this? Or was he just acting on the assumption that Jesus would go along with the consensus and simply rubber-stamp his property claim like everybody else had done? Jesus resented being commandeered into this agreed position as if there were no alternative. He had never before allowed himself to be driven by a desire for money or property; and he didn't intend to be tarnished with that brush now. Jesus had always taught and modelled a different way of living that involved travelling light, being generous, and trusting God for one's daily needs. Jesus knew that if he got sucked into this inheritance dispute, he risked all of that being undermined. If he allowed himself to be co-opted onto one side or the other, it would look like he shared the same materialistic values that motivated everyone else.

These materialistic values give societies two corrupting characteristics:

1. *Materialistic values encourage the acceptance of envy.* The man accosting Jesus was clearly jealous of his brother's wealth and fully expected Jesus to see his envy as a legitimate response to the situation. Although his attitude was at odds with the tenth commandment,[1] he was able to sanitize it as an issue of justice.

---

1. Exodus 20:17

For us today, envy has been sanitized as an essential driver of our modern consumer culture. It is fed by the constant bombardment of celebrity gossip and advertising, so that an insatiable desire for more material goods and the latest product is seen as normal. The escalation of top salaries to such enormous levels is related not so much to individual performance as to comparisons with the pay and benefits of other executives who sit on the company remuneration boards. This is just envy disguised as justice. Writing about the way the LIBOR interest rate had been manipulated for personal and corporate gain, Dan Gledhill, an employee of an American investment bank in London during the late 1990s, wrote: "What's interesting... is the fact that all of us in the dealing room where I worked knew this went on, but simply accepted it. Perhaps we just set the morality bar too low."[2] It is this acceptance of greed and envy as being normal that Jesus finds so offensive.

2. *Materialistic values discourage the asking of questions.* On the face of it, the claim by the man in Luke 12 to what he thinks is rightfully his doesn't seem that unreasonable, especially when viewed from the perspective of our own culture of entitlement in which everyone is conscious of their rights. But this should prompt us to look behind the superficial facts and ask some deeper questions. For example: how did the man's father acquire the property in the first place? Was it taken from small farmers driven into poverty by mounting debts? Was exploitation involved? And why should unearned inherited wealth take precedence over all other social concerns anyway? It is questions like these that we need to ask of *our own* society, rather than blindly accepting what's going on as automatically normal and right. After all, we used to blindly accept that practices in our banking system were normal and right, but we know differently now!

2. *The Independent,* 29 June 2011.

All of this prepares the way for Jesus' parable. He has already demonstrated the need to resist the materialistic pressures of the surrounding culture and to ask questions of practices that are simply taken for granted. Now, Jesus goes on to show the kind of lifestyle he is looking for by telling a story that parodies its exact opposite. The story powerfully highlights the man's lack of three crucial qualities.

1. *Imagination.* It's clear that the rich farmer in the parable has no imagination whatsoever. After being blessed with a bumper harvest, and asking himself, "What shall I do? I have no place to store my crops?" (v17)—the only answer he can come up with is to tear down his barns to build bigger ones. How sad! The conditioning of the surrounding culture was so strong that all he can think of is looking after number one and accumulating as much as he can. It never crossed his mind that there might be other, more noble things he could do with his surplus; for example, giving it to those less fortunate than himself or using it to fund a building or a project that would benefit his community. And it's this same lack of imagination that infects our own thinking about the environment. We are conditioned to assume that there is simply no alternative to the lifestyle we are currently living. We know this lifestyle requires huge amounts of energy, creates lots of waste and pollution, and damages nature; but what can we do? It's just the way things are.

   This shrug of the shoulders is, of course, very convenient because deep down we don't really want to change our lifestyle. That's why we place so much hope in technology. We say: "Isn't it good that engineers are reducing levels of vehicle emissions; that architects are improving the insulation of buildings; that scientists are developing alternative sources of power." And it *is* good. The trouble is that focusing on these advances allows us to avoid making any significant change to the way we live. We continue to consume large

85

amounts of energy, and comfort ourselves that some of it is *green* energy. We continue to take more and more flights, building more and more runways, and comfort ourselves that the planes are becoming more fuel efficient than they used to be. We support "sustainable development" because we think it means we can sustain not just the environment, but our current standard of living as well.

This chapter began with a short sketch about a waiter wanting to pour champagne into a cracked wine glass. It was written to illustrate Jesus' teaching about the folly of putting new wine into old wineskins. Stiffened by frequent use, old skins are liable to burst, argued Jesus; much better to put new wine into new skins. He was making the point that the new life he offered would be jeopardised if people tried to contain it within the old traditions of the Jewish religion. Maybe the same is true when it comes to a new attitude to God's Creation. Big corporations want us to think we can still be concerned for the environment while continuing to buy their products. They flaunt their green credentials as if adding the word "eco" or "natural" to a product's label will render its purchase ecologically beneficial. Clearly BP believed that by changing its name to "*Beyond* Petroleum" and using a pretty sunflower logo it could encourage people to see it *not* as a massive, profit-driven, earth and sea polluting, multi-national oil company; but rather as one of Mother Nature's best friends. But should we be pouring the new wine of our creation concern into the old wineskins of free-market capitalism? Surely an economic system that depends on people acting in self-interest, on companies maximising profits, and on governments chasing continuous growth, is hardly the best system to champion the care of a finite planet. And yet this is the path we are being taken down.

According to Owen Paterson, until recently the UK Environment Secretary, "We shouldn't have to choose between either improving the environment or growing the economy. We should aim to have both..."[3] The first priority recommendation in the March 2013 Final Report of his department's "Ecosystem Markets Task Force" (whose members are all drawn from the world of business) is to allow developers to build on nature reserves or other protected areas so long as they offset the damage done by paying for a similar area to be created elsewhere.[4] While the report makes some good points—about promoting a "circular economy" rather than a "take-make-discard" one, for example—there is something very disturbing about the way it treats nature as simply another commodity in the market place. As Harvey Cox put it:

> For millennia of human history, land has held multiple meanings for human beings—as soil, resting place of the ancestors, holy mountain or enchanted forest, tribal homeland, aesthetic inspiration, sacred turf. The market transforms all these complex meanings into one: land becomes real estate; there is no land that is not theoretically for sale, at the right price.[5]

In a world fixated with economic growth, should we just accept that the best we can hope for is to make companies factor into their calculations the monetary value of all natural resources they use or affect? Would the rich farmer's proposal to tear down his barns and build bigger ones have been acceptable so long as he offset the value of the environment he thereby destroyed? How can we be sure that the market will allow for all the different ways that a piece of nature enriches our lives and, if preserved, would enrich the lives of our descendants?

3. Quoted in *The Telegraph*, 21 April 2013, "Developers can build on nature reserves - if they 'offset' the damage elsewhere, says Government review". `http://bit.ly/11smWZ1`.
4. `http://bit.ly/1clZvJD` (*Ecosystem Makets Task Force Final Report*, DEFRA)
5. Quoted in Celia Deane-Drummond, *Ecotheology*, London: Darton, Longman and Todd, 2008, p. 18.

This is why we need *imagination*. Surely it is possible to do things differently? Can we not set up or join a local cooperative or other community project? Can we not establish or support a Transition Town initiative?[6] Aren't there local farmers who care about the land whom we can support rather than simply buying from the big supermarkets? Many organisations already exist that allow people to pay a regular amount every month to guarantee a farmer's income in return for a box of locally grown vegetables. Such arrangements not only encourage healthier diets but also strengthen communities and re-connect them with where their food comes from. It may not be possible to break free completely from the iron grip that big business and the expanding supermarkets exercise over our towns and cities, but that shouldn't stop us from trying to be more creative in devising better "wineskins" for the new wine of our growing concern for God's creation.

2. *Motivation.* When we hear the man saying to himself in v19, "You have plenty of good things laid up for many years. Take life easy; eat, drink and be merry," we feel like grabbing him by the lapels and shouting, "Is that all you want out of life—just to laze about day after day doing nothing of consequence? Haven't you got any ambition to do something useful or significant for your community? Don't you want to leave some example or legacy for future generations?" Unfortunately, today's society seems to foster the same kind of diluted motivation. We see it in the aspirations expressed by young people. When over a thousand teenagers were asked in a 2010 survey "What would you like to do for your career?" over half of them said they wanted to become a celebrity. Of these, 68% were unsure how they would achieve this, while 5% said they would do so by dating a celebrity.[7] This presents those of us who are concerned for the environment with a serious challenge. Somehow, we have to get people of all ages excited

6. http://www.transitionnetwork.org/
7. *The Independent*, 17 Feb 2010.

about God's Creation. We need to encourage parents, when they have free time, to take their children to the countryside rather than to the shopping centre. We need to testify to how good it feels to be close to nature; to care for it, to restore it, to cultivate it. We need to learn from, and maybe work with, others who are passionate about Nature—the charities and the pressure groups, enlightened local authorities and community organisations. As Christians, we have a lot to offer this coalition for the environment since we believe in a God who has called us to be both stewards and servants of his Creation.

3. *Wisdom.* When God said to the man in Jesus' parable, "You fool!" (v20), it was not so much an insult as a judgment on his way of thinking. It was a judgment that Jesus' listeners would have recognised immediately, because the contrast between foolishness and wisdom is a constant theme throughout their Jewish Scriptures, especially Psalms, Proverbs and Ecclesiastes. Two psalms (14, 53) begin with the statement, "The fool says in his heart 'there is no God'," and it's that same observation that is being applied to the man in the story: He is a fool because he says in his heart "There is no God—I can do whatever I like with my bumper crop; my life is my own and I have complete control over my future". He was wrong, of course. He could use the latest technology to build the biggest barn for storing his surplus grain; but, if God decided his time was up, that was it. "This very night your life will be demanded from you. Then who will get what you have prepared for yourself?" (v20). The rich man didn't have the wisdom to realize what was truly important in life.

Like that rich man, our Western capitalist civilisation has also produced a bumper crop. It has created massive commercial profits, major advances in science and technology, and impressive achievements in culture and communication; but the question is: at a time when millions of people still live in poverty and when the planet's life support systems are dangerously stretched, what shall we do? Will we in the West continue to, "tear down [our barns] and build bigger ones," so that we, "have plenty of good things laid up for many years [and can] take life easy; eat, drink and be merry"? If we do that, then we place our world at risk of being struck by an ecological disaster just as suddenly as the man in the parable was struck down by death.

Or will we recognise that the fear of the Lord is the beginning of wisdom;[8] and that fearing God means using our bumper crop in a way that is consistent with our God-given responsibilities both to the earth and to the poor. To do this will require us to resist the conforming pressures of the consumer culture around us, to question our society's assumptions about what is normal and right, and to rediscover our God-given imagination, motivation, and wisdom.

8. Proverbs 1:7

The Barren Slopes

John 6:1–15

Some time after this, Jesus crossed to the far shore of the Sea of Galilee (that is, the Sea of Tiberias), and a great crowd of people followed him because they saw the signs he had performed by healing the sick. Then Jesus went up on a mountainside and sat down with his disciples. The Jewish Passover Festival was near.

When Jesus looked up and saw a great crowd coming toward him, he said to Philip, "Where shall we buy bread for these people to eat?" He asked this only to test him, for he already had in mind what he was going to do. Philip answered him, "It would take more than half a year's wages to buy enough bread for each one to have a bite!" Another of his disciples, Andrew, Simon Peter's brother, spoke up, "Here is a boy with five small barley loaves and two small fish, but how far will they go among so many?"

Jesus said, "Have the people sit down." There was plenty of grass in that place, and they sat down (about five thousand men were there). Jesus then took the loaves, gave thanks, and distributed to those who were seated as much as they wanted. He did the same with the fish. When they had all had enough to eat, he said to his disciples, "Gather the pieces that are left over. Let nothing be wasted." So they gathered them and filled twelve baskets with the pieces of the five barley loaves left over by those who had eaten.

After the people saw the sign Jesus performed, they began to say, "Surely this is the Prophet who is to come into the world." Jesus, knowing that they intended to come and make him king by force, withdrew again to a mountain by himself.

"Feed the world" was the chorus of the 1984 Band Aid song *Do they know it's Christmas?* Sales of that record, plus the income generated from the associated Live Aid concert, raised £40 million for famine relief. It was a great achievement, but still fell a long way short of what was required. In 2011, the World Food Programme spent *twenty times* that amount buying food for hungry people[1] and it was still nowhere near enough to meet the massive need. In the face of such sobering realities, it's tempting to ask, "What's the point?" That was the reaction Jesus encountered when, sitting on the barren slopes of a mountain, he invited *his* Band Aid disciples to "feed the crowd". "Eight months wages wouldn't buy enough bread for each one to have a bite," says Philip in v7. In other words, "The situation is hopeless, so what's the point?"

It is tempting for us to react the same way as we face the problems of climate change and environmental damage. We know we ought to make our lives more 'green,' but is there really any point? What difference will it make if I drive my car less to cut back on greenhouse gas emissions when over a thousand new coal-fired power stations are being planned worldwide?[2] Why should I bother trying to cut back on the number of plastic carrier bags I use while shopping when a study has shown that 2012 saw a 1.3% increase in single-use plastic bags given out by supermarkets compared with 2011?[3] What's the point of giving up air travel if the same planes will fly whether I'm sitting in them or not? Why am I making such sacrifices if the result of everything I do is just a drop in the ocean?

Traditionally, the story of the feeding of the five thousand has been used to encourage us to believe that, despite the

1. $1.25 billion. See http://bit.ly/1f9csCu ("Record food purchases from developing nations helps UN agency save more lives", World Food Programme)
2. http://bit.ly/1clZvZZ ("More than 1,000 new coal plants planned worldwide, figures show", *The Guardian*).
3. *The Independent*, 19 July 2013. This is on top of an increase of 400 million bags on the year before (see *The Independent*, 5 July 2012).

size of the problem, our small offering can still make a difference. John's version particularly lends itself to this message because it introduces the rather romantic image of a small boy presenting his lunch box. This boy's offering is pathetically small and yet Jesus is still able to use it to feed five thousand people *and* produce twelve baskets full of leftovers! The implication is that Jesus can also do great things with what we bring to him, however puny it may seem. Many other scriptures support this teaching; for example, the moving of mountains with faith as small as a mustard seed, defeating a vast army with just 300 men, and surviving a drought with just a handful of flour and a drop of oil.[4]

Even those who don't believe in miracles find the story of the feeding of the five thousand helpful. For them, the small boy's example encouraged others in the crowd to share the small amounts of food they too had brought. However, whether we attribute the end result to the multiplying effect of Christ's power or to the ripple effect of the boy's example, the moral of the story is still the same: we must do what we can, however small it may seem when compared to the size of the problem.

The trouble is that the environmental destruction and global warming we face today is of a wholly different order of *magnitude*. The story's ratio of five loaves to five thousand people may seem pretty big, but it is totally overshadowed by the ratio between, say, my greenhouse gas emissions and global emissions. Even if I manage to *halve* the amount of carbon dioxide I produce to 2½ tons a year (which would take some doing) what is that compared to the 1000 tons *a second* that the world is pumping into the atmosphere?[5] I may offset my holiday flight by paying for a few trees to be planted, but what is that compared to an area the size of England and Wales being cleared from the world's tropical rain forests

4. Matthew 17:20; Judges 7; 2 Kings 4:1-7
5. James Garvey, "Climate Change and Causal Inefficacy" in O'Hear, A. (ed.) *Philosophy and the Environment*, Royal Institute of Philosophy Supplement 69, p. 160.

every year?[6] In other words, the mountain *we* face is far larger and its slopes far more barren than was the mountain on which the five thousand were fed.

As well as magnitude, we also face a wholly different order of *complexity*. Jesus' disciples were presented with a straight forward causal connection between a problem and its solution. The people were hungry because they had insufficient food; give them more food and the problem is solved. Unfortunately, our ecological crisis cannot be reduced to such a simple equation. There are a multitude of factors that interact with each other in so many ways. A change in one variable—say, the temperature of seawater—may lead to changes in the height of the sea level, the strength and direction of ocean currents, the rate of algae formation, the amount of water vapour in the atmosphere, and a host of other things... *or it may not*, since there are all kinds of feedback loops that can balance out one change by another. Even using the world's most powerful computers, scientists are still struggling to explain all the ways in which the earth, the oceans, the atmosphere, the plants and the animals affect each other. So, while we might be able to make a connection between a donation of loaves and fish with the relief of someone's hunger; we have no way of knowing whether our decision to cycle rather than drive to work will lead to a reduction of drought in East Africa or of flooding in Bangladesh.

These issues of magnitude and complexity create a dilemma if we try to follow what philosophers call a *consequentialist* approach to ethical living, which we all do to some extent. This involves performing good actions because we can see or imagine the beneficial consequences those actions will have. Like the boy in the story, we offer our gifts and skills, however small they might be, because we believe they will improve the lives of others. But, when it comes to doing things for the

6. http://bit.ly/1clZtBi ("Rainforest Facts and Figures", The Rainforest Foundation)

sake of *the environment*, this belief is more difficult to sustain. Two examples will illustrate the problem:

- Suppose we choose to buy more local produce in order to reduce food-miles and the associated greenhouse gas emissions. How can we measure the effect this is having?

  And, what about fair-trade goods? Are the benefits of reduced pollution cancelled out by the detrimental effect that fewer food-miles would have on poor farmers in developing countries whose livelihood depends on their exports?

- Or suppose we decided to press for the construction of more nuclear power stations because this would reduce our nation's dependence on greenhouse gas producing coal and oil-fired stations. Do the benefits of this outweigh the dangers of storing greater amounts of nuclear waste? And how sure can we be that the world's rising demand for energy won't result in such nuclear stations simply being *added* to coal and gas-fired ones rather than replacing them?

When we realize just how huge and complex the environmental problems that face us are, it isn't surprising that we are tempted to shrug our shoulders and say, "What's the point?" When people can't see what their green actions are actually achieving, it's very difficult to find the motivation to keep doing them. But that's where John's account of the Feeding of the Five Thousand comes to our aid.

It is crucial that we recognise the significant differences between John's version of the story and those of Matthew, Mark and Luke.

1. John makes explicit the link between this feeding miracle and the Exodus from Egypt. Most Jewish readers would pick up the hints whichever gospel they were reading. The bread that Jesus miraculously multiplied for the crowd mirrored the

manna that God had miraculously provided for their ancestors. The twelve basketfuls gathered up afterwards reminded them of the twelve tribes God gathered to himself at Mount Sinai before leading them through the wilderness. But John makes doubly sure that his readers make this connection by stating right at the start of his account: "The Jewish Passover Feast was near" (v4). He wants everyone to relate the Feeding of the Five Thousand directly to the event that founded the Jewish nation.

2. John makes explicit the link between the Feeding of the Five Thousand and the Last Supper. The hint is there in all of the Gospel accounts when Jesus takes the bread, gives thanks and breaks it, just as he would later do at that Passover meal the night before he died. But John goes on in chapter 6 to underline the connection by quoting Jesus as saying things like: "This bread is my flesh which I will give for the life of the world" (v51).

3. John reverses the direction of the initial challenge. In Matthew, Mark and Luke, it is the disciples who see how long the people have gone without eating and challenge Jesus to send them away to buy food. In John, it is Jesus who sees the crowd and challenges his disciple, "Where shall we buy bread for these people to eat?" (v5). And what is more, he does so even before the crowd has arrived. The need hasn't even presented itself yet and already Jesus is looking for a response.

The effect of all these variations to the story is to shift the emphasis away from *consequentialism* and towards what philosophers call *virtue ethics*. The challenge facing the disciples, according to John, was to respond to the needs of the crowd not by working out the beneficial consequences of their activity, but by *living out the benevolent characteristics of their identity*. By emphasising the Passover, John is reminding the Jewish readers of his gospel *who they are*. Just like those disciples, they were members of a people that God had rescued from the unequal society of slaves and masters and brought into a new life of compassion and justice; into a community in which there was enough manna for everyone. Therefore, they shouldn't share their loaves and fishes just because of its beneficial consequences; they should share them because *that's the kind of people they are.* By stressing the Last Supper, John is making this identity issue even more pertinent for Christians. He is telling us that even if we don't have faith for a miracle, and even if we don't see our good deeds achieving very much, *we should still do them* because, in the words of another apostle, we are "a chosen people, a royal priesthood, a holy nation, a people belonging to God [to] declare the praises of him who called [us] out of darkness into his wonderful light."[7] It's not that we shouldn't be spurred on by the hope of making a difference; it's just that our prime motivation needs to be *to live out who we are*; because without this deeper source of motivation we will struggle to keep going during those times when our actions produce few results.

In other words, if our motivation for "going green" is over-dependent on the hope of seeing results, we will soon lose heart and cry, "What's the point?" The problems associated with environmental destruction and climate change are so huge and so complex that it is almost impossible to directly link any progress we may (hopefully) see on the global scene with any of the individual actions we undertake from day to day. But that doesn't mean we should stop doing them. We don't just act because of what it might achieve; we act because of who we are. It's rather like voting. Of course we vote because we want to see a preferred candidate elected. But we also vote because of who we are—people who believe in democracy; who treasure and uphold freedom and justice; and who wish to honour the sacrifices of those who made it possible for us to be citizens rather than subjects. Voting is an expression of our values and principles; not just a mechanism for gaining certain results. It's still a good thing to do *even if* our preferred

7. 1 Peter 2:9

candidate has no hope of getting in. The same is true for our environmentally friendly actions; they are an expression of our values and principles. We do them to remain true to ourselves; we do them to be consistent, to be whole. We are glad when they *do* achieve the results we hope for; but we still do them even when they don't or when it's impossible to tell. That's why we should continue to shun disposable plastic bags *even though* the total numbers issued by supermarkets has gone up rather than down. That's why we should continue to cut down our own greenhouse gas emissions *even though* the global figures are still rising. That's why we should continue recycling our waste, continue conserving water and energy, continue preserving natural habitats for wildlife and continue living simple lives uncluttered by possessions... because all of these things express who we are.

We mustn't forget, of course, that at the end of the story of the Feeding of the Five Thousand, the miraculous *did* happen—the five thousand *were* fed! It's true that the magnitude and complexity of the problems facing us today are much greater than those which faced the first disciples, and we may wonder whether the Jesus who enabled his disciples to "feed the crowd" *then* is powerful enough to enable us to "feed the world" *now*. As if to re-assure us on this, immediately after describing the crowd being fed, John decides to insert the story of Jesus walking on the water. Maybe he thought: "The long discussion about Jesus being the bread of life can wait for a moment; what my readers need to know *now* is that this Jesus who fed 5000 people is none other than the Almighty Creator—the One who made the earth, sea and sky." He is the one who, according to Psalm 104, rebukes the waters and feeds not just the five thousand but *all* the earth's animals.[8]

It is the same Jesus who walks towards *us* across the waters of ecological chaos to bring his peace[9]. It's a peace that enables

8. Psalm 104:7,27
9. John 6:19-21

us to keep going, to keep praying, and to keep caring for his world; motivated not just by the prospect of achieving great things in his strength, but also by the desire to *be* the people he has called us to be—people who care about justice, about beauty, about compassion, about the needs of the poor and of future generations, about the wonder and diversity of creation... in fact, about everything that *God* cares about. The story ends with Jesus withdrawing so that people couldn't make him king by force (v15). It reminds us that we can't force Jesus to solve all our world's problems just like that. Instead, however barren are the mountain slopes we find ourselves on, we must continue to do what we can and, more importantly, continue to be the people he has called us to be. The rest, thankfully, is up to him.

The Mysterious Cloud

Matthew 17:1–8

After six days Jesus took with him Peter, James and John the brother of James, and led them up a high mountain by themselves. There he was transfigured before them. His face shone like the sun, and his clothes became as white as the light. Just then there appeared before them Moses and Elijah, talking with Jesus.

Peter said to Jesus, "Lord, it is good for us to be here. If you wish, I will put up three shelters—one for you, one for Moses and one for Elijah."

While he was still speaking, a bright cloud covered them, and a voice from the cloud said, "This is my Son, whom I love; with him I am well pleased. Listen to him!"

When the disciples heard this, they fell face down to the ground, terrified. But Jesus came and touched them. "Get up," he said. "Don't be afraid." When they looked up, they saw no one except Jesus.

Romans 10:33–11:2

Oh, the depth of the riches of the wisdom and knowl-
edge of God!
How unsearchable his judgments,
and his paths beyond tracing out!
"Who has known the mind of the Lord?
Or who has been his counsellor?"

> "Who has ever given to God,
>   that God should repay them?"
> For from him and through him and for him are all
>   things.
>   To him be the glory forever! Amen.

Therefore, I urge you, brothers and sisters, in view of God's mercy, to offer your bodies as a living sacrifice, holy and pleasing to God— this is your true and proper worship. Do not conform to the pattern of this world, but be transformed by the renewing of your mind. Then you will be able to test and approve what God's will is—his good, pleasing and perfect will.

Clouds are the result of the invisible becoming visible. Normally, we cannot see the water vapour in the air around us, but when air rises and cools, the vapour it contains starts to condense around minute dust particles to form water droplets. Since billions of these droplets together refract and reflect the sunlight, the resulting cloud takes shape before our eyes. This process makes clouds an ideal symbol for those moments when the invisible God reveals his presence in a tangible way. It was through a cloud that God spoke to Noah, Moses and Ezekiel.[1] It was by a cloud that God led the Israelites in the wilderness and hallowed their temple.[2] It was from the clouds that the Jews were encouraged to expect God's future Messiah to appear.[3]

Also, because clouds are enigmatic, having both positive and negative connotations, it makes them a suitable image to convey the mystery of the divine. Clouds can offer life-giving rain and the blessing of shade on a hot day; but they can also bring gloom, storms and floods. They, like the God who "rides upon them,"[4] must be treated with respect.

1. Genesis 9:13; Exodus 33:9; Ezekiel 1:4
2. Exodus 40:36-37; 1 Kings 8:10-11
3. Daniel 7:13
4. Psalms 18:9; 68:4; 104:3; Isaiah 19:1

So when Peter, on the Mount of Transfiguration, presumed to give Jesus his knee-jerk suggestion for preserving the divine splendour in some hastily erected shelters, it was a voice from a cloud that silenced him. It was through that mysterious cloud that God reminded the disciples that Jesus was there to be listened to, not controlled (Matthew 17:5).

All of this has particular relevance to our current environmental situation. Jesus himself extended the symbolism of the cloud to include God speaking through the natural and political events of his day. "When you see a cloud rising in the west" he told a crowd, "immediately you say, 'It's going to rain,' and it does... Hypocrites! You know how to interpret the appearance of the earth and sky. How is it that you don't know how to interpret this present time?"[5] His comment was followed by a reference to two recent tragedies and a parable about an unfruitful fig tree. Jesus was underlining the need for his listeners to take what was happening around them seriously and act accordingly, for ..."unless you repent, you too will all perish."[6] How do we take what is happening to our environment seriously? How do we make good decisions that will avoid us, and the other inhabitants of our endangered world, perishing?

In his letter to the Romans, the Apostle Paul offers some valuable guidelines. The relevant passage (11:33–12:2) occurs at that pivotal point found in many of Paul's letters when he moves from explaining doctrine to describing lifestyle. For the first eleven chapters of Romans, Paul has been teaching his readers the things they should *believe*: that they are saved by faith not law, that they have been united in Christ's death and resurrection through baptism, that the Holy Spirit gives freedom, that God loves Gentiles and Jews equally, and—of particular relevance to our current environmental crisis—that "creation itself would one day be set free from its slavery

5. Luke 12:54-56.
6. Luke 13:3,5

103

to decay and share the glorious freedom of the children of God."[7]. In the final four chapters Paul spells out the kinds of behaviour that those beliefs should inspire. Our passage lies at the turning point between these two sections, and contains three principles about translating theological understanding into practical decision-making that we must act on if we are to respond appropriately to the ecological issues we face.

1. *We must adopt a humble approach.* At first sight, our passage appears to contradict itself. It begins in 11:33 by saying, "Oh, the depth of the riches of the wisdom and knowledge of God! How unsearchable his judgments, and his paths beyond tracing out!" This implies that God's thoughts and ways cannot be understood by humans. And yet, the passage ends by saying, "Then you will be able to test and approve what God's will is— his good, pleasing and perfect will" (12:2). How can God's wisdom be both beyond us and available to us; how can God's ways be both unfathomable and knowable? Once again we are facing the mysterious cloud, the same one that enveloped the disciples on the Mount of Transfiguration. One minute, they were looking at their teacher's familiar face; the next, they are blinded by its dazzling glory. One moment, a loud voice from the cloud throws them to the ground in terror; the next, a soft voice from their teacher says, "Get up. Don't be afraid." Maybe the experience was a timely reminder to the disciples not to become over-familiar. However much they thought they understood Jesus, there would always be something mysterious and unpredictable about him. The same is true for God's Creation. However much we learn about our planet; however much we try to control it with science and technology; there will always be something mysterious and unpredictable about the forces of Nature. As Paul reminds us, those forces were not meant to conform to *our* limited mental capacities; rather, "from *him* and through *him* and to *him* are all things. To *him* be the glory for ever! Amen" (v36).

7. Romans 8:21 GNB

Maintaining this wider perspective on Creation is crucial when we try to discern the will of God for living environmentally friendly lives. It warns us not to reduce everything to a simplistic formula. I think Paul is aware of this danger when he introduces the image of temple sacrifice in 12:1. He knows that this image will tempt his readers to think of rules, hierarchies and obligations, because that had often been their experience of temple worship —religious leaders telling them what God requires, how to obtain his favour, how to live.

That is *not* the message Paul wants to communicate here, and so he takes care to set it within the context of God's incomprehensible wisdom and of a vast universe that makes any man-made temple look like a mere speck of dust by comparison. He quotes from the Book of Job: "Who has ever given to God, that God should repay him?" (11:35) to undermine any idea that God is somehow obligated to bless us if we follow certain instructions.

Paul wants to demonstrate that discerning God's will is not a matter of simply obeying rules and practices laid down by someone else—even if that someone else is a great Christian preacher or a passionate environmental activist. In the face of the mystery and complexity of God's Creation, making decisions about how we should live calls for a spirit of humility. It would be totally inappropriate for anyone to say: "God says you must give up flying," or "God says you must stop eating meat," or "God says you must always buy second-hand".

That was the approach of the Pharisees. *They* thought they understood God's will for society so perfectly that it gave them the right to legislate on every aspect of people's lives. Paul was aware of that temptation—after all, he used to be a Pharisee! But, since his conversion, he had come to realize just, "how unsearchable [are God's] judgments, and his paths beyond tracing out" (11:33). And it's the same with the size and complexity of the ecological issues we face; they cannot simply be reduced to a list of rules, however sensible those rules might be. Each one of us must come before God daily and, in the light of what we've learnt about his Creation, humbly ask; "How then do you want me to live?" Heaven does not produce an accredited list of shops to buy from. The Bible doesn't stipulate the thickness of insulation to be used in our loft; nor does it issue a blanket moratorium on air transport. Furthermore, heaven won't allow us to impose such stipulations on others. Instead, Jesus simply says, "Follow me, and let's work out the environmental implications of your discipleship as we go along."

2. *We must consider the common good.* Here we return to Paul's instruction in 12:1 to, "offer yourselves as a living sacrifice." I have used the Good News Version here because unfortunately the New International Version has succumbed to a common mis-translation of Paul's word for sacrifice that makes it plural when it should be singular. The bodies we offer are many, but together they become one corporate sacrifice. Paul is challenging us to live our individual lives in such a way that they enable our whole community to become a living sacrifice. This corporate goal is reinforced by the remainder of chapter 12 which teaches that each person should use their individual gifts, love, zeal and hospitality to build up the united body and witness of the church.

Surely such a focus on the common good is fundamental to how we make decisions that have a bearing on the environment. After all, the environment is not just ours, it's everyone's. The earth does not exist merely to satisfy the desires of the richest ten per cent of humanity, it is there to meet the needs of all living creatures.

The problem is that our individualistic consumer culture encourages us to indulge the "private me" that screams "I want!" at the expense of the "public me" that says "We need."[8] The "private me" dominated our childhood, but as

8. This terminology comes from Benjamin R Barber, *Consumed*, New York: W. W. Norton & Co, 2007, pp. 128-144.

we grew and matured, we learnt to subordinate its desires to the needs of the wider community. We realized that it was actually in our interest that *everyone* prospers. So we pay our taxes, we volunteer our time, we put our litter in the bin. Unfortunately, the modern marketing of consumer goods combined with unfettered privatization are deliberately aimed at turning us back into indulged children; making us believe that we deserve, and can have, anything we want. Such a situation is fatal for our environment because its health depends on individuals looking *beyond* their own private wants and making decisions that promote the common good. Paul calls us to "offer ourselves" (which involves letting go of our own desires) so that *our community* may become "a living sacrifice, holy and pleasing to God."

One of the sessions at the 2012 Hay Literature Festival featured a panel of environmental experts who were asked by a member of the audience during the question time, to say when each of them had last used air transport and why. Sitting in the audience I could feel the panel's embarrassment, and yet their answers were very revealing. One admitted he had recently flown to Malaysia for a conference about rainforest clearance. Another confessed he had flown to Canada with his elderly mother because that was the only way she could see her other son who now lived there. I realized that although I opposed unnecessary flying because of the large amounts of green-house gases it adds to the atmosphere, I could see the common good that would result from attending an international conference on rainforests or preserving a mother-son relationship across the ocean. It reminded me that we are not called to be ecological Pharisees imposing our own laws about flying and other environmentally sensitive activities on other people; rather we should debate the issues with humility and with a concern for the common good.

3. *We must apply a transformed mind.* Paul writes in v2, "Do not conform any longer to the pattern of this world, but be transformed by the renewing of your mind." The Greek word used

here for "transformed" is the same one used for "transfigured" in Matthew 17:2. This connection helps to throw some light on what Paul is trying to say.

Firstly, when Jesus was transfigured / transformed, he suddenly found himself in the presence of Moses and Elijah. According to Luke's version, "they spoke about his departure which he was about to bring to fulfilment at Jerusalem" (9:31). In other words, transformation for Jesus meant being able to see his life within the flow of history; of how he was building on the work of the prophets of previous generations like Moses and Elijah, and how he in turn would provide salvation for future generations.

This is the kind of inward transformation *we* need if we are going to live in an environmentally sustainable way. We must see our lives within the flow of history; acknowledging what we owe to those who have praised and protected nature in the past, and recognising the effects our present actions will have on the future lives of our children and grandchildren. Jesus was willing to sacrifice himself for the good of coming generations, and he calls us to make sacrifices too. This, says Paul, will involve, "a renewing of [our] mind". We must no longer think as our modern consumer culture wants us to think, with its focus on immediate individual gratification. Rather, we should factor the needs of future generations into the decisions we make about goods purchased and energy consumed. Giving honour to our ancestors and consideration to our descendants is a crucial part of the renewing of our mind.

Secondly, Jesus' transformation meant that he and the disciples heard a voice saying, "This is my own dear Son with whom I am pleased—listen to him!" Jesus had heard that same affirmation at his baptism. On both occasions, God was encouraging Jesus to *live out who he was*, even if this involved hardship. And that's what a transformed mind means for us too. It is the "virtue ethic" advocated in the previous chapter. It involves making environmentally-friendly decisions not just because they might have good consequences, but because such decisions reflect who we are—God's own dear son/daughter with whom he is pleased. Which is more compatible with our status as a child of God: a life of wasteful extravagance or one of grateful simplicity? Which is more compatible with who we are in Christ: refusing to take notice of the warnings about global warming or seeking to reduce our carbon footprint?

We are exhorted by Paul not to conform any longer to the self-centred consumerist pattern of this world, but to be transformed by the renewing of our mind so that, in our thinking, we treasure the achievements of past generations, consider the needs of future generations, and generate actions consistent with the kind of people God has created and redeemed us to be. If we respond in this way then we will be able to, "test and approve what God's will is—his good, pleasing and perfect will." We will be able to do this *not* because some preacher or environmental activist has presented us with a list of instructions—the mysterious depths of God and of his creation are too great for that; but because we seek to adopt a humble approach, consider the common good, and apply a transformed mind.

The Restricted Corn

Matthew 12:1–21

At that time Jesus went through the grainfields on the Sabbath. His disciples were hungry and began to pick some heads of grain and eat them. When the Pharisees saw this, they said to him, "Look! Your disciples are doing what is unlawful on the Sabbath." He answered, "Haven't you read what David did when he and his companions were hungry? He entered the house of God, and he and his companions ate the consecrated bread—which was not lawful for them to do, but only for the priests… I tell you that something greater than the temple is here. If you had known what these words mean, 'I desire mercy, not sacrifice,' you would not have condemned the innocent. For the Son of Man is Lord of the Sabbath."

Going on from that place, he went into their synagogue, and a man with a shrivelled hand was there. Looking for a reason to bring charges against Jesus, they asked him, "Is it lawful to heal on the Sabbath?" He said to them, "If any of you has a sheep and it falls into a pit on the Sabbath, will you not take hold of it and lift it out? How much more valuable is a person than a sheep! Therefore it is lawful to do good on the Sabbath."

Then he said to the man, "Stretch out your hand." So he stretched it out and it was completely restored, just as sound as the other. But the Pharisees went out and plotted how they might kill Jesus.

Aware of this, Jesus withdrew from that place. A large crowd followed him, and he healed all who were ill. He warned them not to tell others about him. This was to fulfill what was spoken through the prophet Isaiah:

"Here is my servant whom I have chosen,
    the one I love, in whom I delight;
I will put my Spirit on him,
    and he will proclaim justice to the nations.
He will not quarrel or cry out;
    no one will hear his voice in the streets.
A bruised reed he will not break,
    and a smouldering wick he will not snuff out,
till he has brought justice through to victory.
In his name the nations will put their hope."

Sighting the Slave Ship

We came to unexpected latitudes—
sighted the slave ship
during divine service
on deck.

In earlier dog-days
we had made landfall
between forests of sandlewood,
taken on salt, falcons and sulphur.

What haunted us later
was not the cool dispensing
of sacrament
in the burnished doldrums

but something more exotic--
that sense
of a slight shift of cargo
while becalmed.

Pauline Stainer[1]

1. *Poems*, Tarset: Bloodaxe Books, 2003.

In 2012, Dennis Spurr, the proprietor of the "Fantastic Sausage Factory" in Weymouth, Dorset, had a brilliant idea. His butcher's shop looked out on the harbour where the Olympic sailing events were due to take place so why not create a sign for his window showing the five Olympic rings made entirely out of sausages! Sadly for him, not long after putting up the sign, Sponsorship Enforcement Officers turned up and threatened him with legal action if he didn't remove it. Mr. Spurr wasn't the only victim of the tough Olympic sponsorship rules. There were almost 300 enforcement officers, wearing purple caps and tops, checking businesses across the country to ensure that they were not illegally associating themselves with the Games at the expense of official sponsors such as Adidas, McDonald's, Coca-Cola and BP. These officers had the right to enter shops and offices and take the owners to court if their advertising mentioned any banned words like, "gold", "silver", "bronze", "summer" and "London."

The Pharisees described in Matthew 12 were just like those Olympic Games Enforcement Officers—they were protecting a festival that was intended to bring benefit to the whole of society. Their weekly Sabbath had been designed to promote rest, worship and family-time; just as the four-yearly Olympics were designed to encourage personal achievement, community inspiration and international goodwill. However, because of rising costs, the Olympics acquired an extra aim: to raise money. The London Games cost around £9 billion, and to help cover this, £1.4 billion had to be raised through corporate sponsorship.[2]

The organisers argued that without involving big profit-driven companies and protecting their sponsorship rights, the Games would not have been financially viable. They may have been right, but it felt like a corruption of the *spirit* of the Olympics. We wanted to shout out, "Something greater

2. http://bit.ly/1clZvcz ("London 2012 Olympic sponsors list: who are they and what have they paid?", *The Guardian*, 23 October 2012)

than corporate capitalism is here!" just as Jesus shouted out, "Something greater than the temple is here!" (v6). He knew that the Jerusalem temple had become Israel's economic power-house, converting religious observance into a healthy profit. The money spent by thousands of pilgrims on food, accommodation and sacrifices fuelled the economy, and the Pharisees were determined to keep it that way. That's why they enforced the Sabbath rules so strictly. They had to ensure that their religious influence so saturated people's lives that it was simply accepted as normal.

Big business does the same today. Through mass advertising and sponsorship, it tries to ensure that corporate capitalism so saturates *our* lives that we simply accept it as normal. Nothing must be done to undermine the money-making system. So, just as Mr. Spurr wasn't allowed to make his own Olympic rings out of sausage meat; so the disciples weren't allowed to make their own food out of standing corn. By picking the ears, rubbing them to separate grain from husk, and blowing the husks away, they were deemed to be reaping, threshing and winnowing (albeit on a miniature scale). This was work and it could only be done on days that were sanctioned by the official Sabbath sponsors. It was restricted corn.

The comment, "It's the economy, stupid!" was first used in Bill Clinton's 1992 presidential campaign, and it seems particularly apt today given the severe financial difficulties we face. But maybe what's *really* stupid is to forget what the word "economy" originally meant. It comes from the Greek term for a manager of a household. *Oikos* means 'household' and *nemein* means 'manage'. So, when we talk about the British or the world economy, we are really talking about the management of very large households; and managing any household involves making sure that things run smoothly for the benefit of every member. An economy, therefore, isn't just about finances, it's also about fairness. It's about justice.

During the second half of the 20th century, we were led to believe that if we focused just on the finances, fairness would automatically follow; that if we allowed some members of the household to make a lot of money, the benefits would "trickle down" to all the rest. We were told that if some people were struggling with only a small slice of the cake, the best way to help them was not to get those with bigger slices to share, but to focus on making the whole cake bigger—then everyone would benefit. So that's what we've done; we've concentrated on *growing* the cake rather than *sharing* it, with the result that we are now gobbling up the planet's resources at an alarming rate and the gap between rich and poor has dramatically increased.[3] We are beginning to realize that those who insist on enforcing the present economic system are the ones who benefit from it the most, often at the expense of the poor.

It was the same in Jesus' day. The reason the Pharisees were so keen to enforce the existing religious system was that they were the ones who benefitted from it the most, again often at the expense of the poor. Jesus saw through this and wasn't prepared to tolerate it. He challenged the Pharisees by reminding them that when the soldiers of their hero David were hungry, he fed them with the altar bread despite the religious rules that banned its ordinary use. Jesus then went on to do something similar himself by healing a man's withered hand despite the religious rules that banned such activity on the Sabbath (vs9-14). He also quoted the words of the prophet Hosea, "I desire mercy, not sacrifice." Jesus was making the point that God doesn't approve of any system—religious or economic—that encourages people to be unmerciful. As Jesus would tell the Pharisees on a later occasion: "You give a tenth of your spices—mint, dill and cumin, but you have neglected the more important matters of the Law—justice, mercy and faithfulness."[4]

As Jesus moved among the crowds, his great aim was to bring justice and mercy to every individual he met. However, when

3. Wilkinson & Pickett, *The Spirit Level*, London: Penguin, 2010, especially pp. 239-245.
4. Matthew 23:23

Matthew was writing this down, he decided to add a quotation from Isaiah 42 to show that, for Jesus, justice and mercy weren't just for individuals but for nations as well: "Here is my servant, whom I have chosen... he will proclaim justice *to the nations*... A bruised reed he will not break, and a smouldering wick he will not snuff out, till he leads justice to victory. In his name *the nations* will put their hope."[5] The problem was that the Jews had become so blinded by the religious system that dominated their lives that they failed to see how *un*just and *un*merciful it had made them. And we too can become so blinded by the economic system that dominates *our* lives that we fail to see how unjust and unmerciful it has made *us*.

Pauline Stainer's powerful poem *Sighting the Slave Ship* can be read as an indictment of the Western capitalist mind-set. The poem is set in the 18th century and describes a ship's crew receiving Holy Communion. The fact that they are part of a trading operation that plundered other parts of the world doesn't seem to bother them—it's just the normal way things are. The falcons they've "taken on" represent exploited nature; the sulphur (used to make gunpowder) implies warfare. The poem's speaker does, however, feel vaguely haunted by the sight of an approaching slave ship. He can't explain why it makes him feel uneasy but he puts it down to, "...that sense of a slight shift of cargo while becalmed." The cargo, of course, is live human beings who don't always keep still like boxes and crates. Since this oppression and cruelty is largely kept below deck, it remains unseen and doesn't affect the religious rituals going on above. The crew don't even think about it. It's only when their economic progress has been halted, when their ship has been "becalmed" by entering the doldrums, that this "sense of a slight shift of cargo" can actually be felt.

Maybe that's where *we* are today. Our economic progress has been halted, our Western capitalist economy has been becalmed by entering a recession, and we find ourselves

5. Matthew 12 v17-21 (italics added)

feeling slightly uneasy about what lies below the deck—the destruction of nature, the injustice in our trading systems, the plight of the poor. The speaker in the poem is looking back on the experience. He feels haunted by what he remembers, and maybe also by the fact that he didn't do anything about it. After reading the poem, we are left wondering whether that will be us in a few years' time? Will we also look back and be haunted by the memory of that "sense of a slight shift of cargo"—those moments of revelation that we were part of an unjust and uncaring system which we did nothing about?

The poem also reflects the scenario described in Matthew 12 vs1-21. The Pharisees too were engaged in "divine service on deck," blind to the effect their religious system was having on the poor and sick below. Jesus challenges them to open their eyes to the injustices they were perpetuating; to see that they were treating people as little more than money-making cargo. Jesus effectively draws their attention to the sound of three voices.

1. *The voice of scripture.* The Pharisees claimed to know the Hebrew Scriptures inside out and yet Jesus is appalled at their ignorance. "Haven't you read what David did...?" he asks in v3. This is followed by "Haven't you read in the Law...?" (v5) and, "If you had known what these words [of scripture] mean... you would not have condemned the innocent" (v7). These religious people had been so blinkered in their reading of scripture that they failed to register its countless references to justice and mercy. They had been blinded by their self-serving religious system.

   Our own self-serving *economic* system can have the same effect. We may be very religious. We may think we know our bibles; but we still read them through spectacles borrowed from the consumer culture we live in. Have we *really* understood our God-given responsibilities towards the earth, its people, its animals and plants; to be good stewards and humble servants of God's creation? During the course of this book, we've explored passages from Genesis, Leviticus, Numbers, Psalms, Job, Isaiah, the Gospels and Paul's letters; but have we really taken on board the strength of God's love for all he has made; his concern for land, for the rights of animals, for ethical living, and for future generations? Or have we allowed the Enforcement Officers of consumer capitalism—the advertisers, the media, the corporations, the politicians—to drown out the voice of scripture and tempt us to carry on with business as usual? Have we been haunted by "that sense of a slight shift in cargo" over recent months and yet done nothing?

2. *The voice of the heretic.* We mustn't overlook the fact that, in our passage, Jesus is being a heretic. He questions what everyone else accepted as normal. "I tell you" he says in v6, "that something greater than the temple is here." This was heresy as far as the establishment was concerned; what could be greater than the temple! Jesus then goes on to advocate breaking the temple's rules for the sake of a greater good. He points out that some of their rules betrayed the spirit in which the original Law was given. The Sabbath was never meant to stand in the way of healing a man's withered hand.

We in 21st century church and society must make space for heretical voices because they provoke us to re-examine what we take for granted. Why do we accept as normal a lifestyle that requires for its continuation the unsustainable exploitation of the earth's resources and the unjust impoverishment of half the world's population? Why, when we shop for food, do we instinctively follow the capitalist mantra and demand the cheapest prices, the greatest choice, and instant availability?

What if we heard a voice telling us to be willing to pay *more* money, to be satisfied with *less* choice, and to do without food that isn't locally in season? We would think that voice was crazy. But maybe what is really crazy is to continue with an economic system that provides cheapness, choice and availability at the cost of more forests being felled, more wildlife losing its habitat, more workers in poor countries being exploited, and more small, environmentally-conscious growers being driven out of business.

The heretical voice will often come from a contemporary artist whose work shocks us into seeing things from a new perspective. Figure 5 on the following page shows a cartoon by the illustrator David Parkins. It presents a powerful image of a world wrung dry of its oil and, by implication, of its other resources. It appears to be happening in order to satisfy the greed of humans, who are seen pushing and shoving each other just to obtain the last few drops. While every nationality is represented, not a single face in the picture expresses happiness or contentment; they are all distorted with rage or anxiety. Neither is a single hand open; they are all grasping, with fingers bent and knuckles protruding. The cartoon, as well as forcing us to face the social and environmental consequences of our lust for oil and other resources, also raises a crucial question: whose hands are doing the wringing? They are drawn reaching down from above the picture space as if they belonged to God.

Such an implication is disturbing for Christians and others who want to believe the reassuring words sung since childhood: "He's got the whole world in his hands." Being held in God's hands has always meant a world being cared for, not throttled; so how can the descending hands in the cartoon belong to God? If they do, then perhaps this is God "giving [us] over" to reap the consequences of our "depraved mind."[6] However, it's more likely that the artist wants us to see these as the hands of someone we have foolishly made into a god. The hands of the true God are open hands—open to satisfy all earth's creatures with good things;[7] open to receive the prodigal son;[8] open to suffer the nails of crucifixion. The pictured

6. Romans 1:28-32
7. Psalm 104:28
8. Luke 15:20

Figure 5: David Parkins, *Oil*

hands, however, look like exaggerated versions of the grasping hands of the people below; the same bent fingers, the same protruding knuckles. These hands therefore seem to represent the capitalist god of big business; the god who gives us what we crave for even when it is bad for us and bad for the earth.

The picture is therefore a challenge: are we going to be one of the crowd desperately waving our container in the hope of catching enough drops to keep our energy-guzzling lifestyle going for a bit longer? Or are we going to be shocked by the visual provocation of a heretic into having a re-think? Creation is indeed groaning; and contemporary artists like David Parkins are pointing this out using the same heretical 'voice' that we've heard from the likes of Rachel Carson[9], Franz Schumacher[10], James Lovelock[11], Swampy[12], Caroline Lucas[13] and Jonathan Porritt[14].

An openness to heretical voices is also crucial within the environmental movement itself. Jesus announced that, "Something greater than the temple is here." I think he would also say, "Something greater than the *environment* is here." For people like me, this is a difficult pill to swallow. The environmental movement can become a kind of temple, a holy cause that cannot be criticised—like motherhood and apple pie. But environmental activists can be just as guilty of perpetuating injustice as anyone else. They can, for example, place so much emphasis on reducing global CO_2 emissions that they resemble the Pharisees protecting the Sabbath at

9. See Rachel Carson, *Silent Spring*, London: Penguin Classics, 1965, credited by many for helping to launch the modern environment movement.
10. See E. F. Schumacher, *Small is beautiful*, first published London: Blond & Briggs, 1973; a classic critique of the policies of big business.
11. See Lovelock's various books that unpack the implications of his Gaia hypothesis
12. The nickname of the "eco-warrior" Daniel Hooper who gained publicity in the 1990s by living in tunnels to prevent the construction of the Newbury bypass and a second runway for Manchester airport.
13. Former leader of the Green Party and now a Green Party MP.
14. Former director of Friends of the Earth.

any price. Maybe Jesus would also say "Something greater than CO_2 is here; what about justice and mercy?" Are we in the rich industrialised countries going to compensate the poorer nations for all the CO_2 we have *already* pumped into the atmosphere? Are we going to allow multi-national companies to make huge profits developing the technology to limit the effects of global warming when it was their drive for huge profits that helped to cause the global warming in the first place? Is the crusade to reduce CO_2 so sacrosanct that it justifies turning more and more farmland over to bio-fuels in a time of global grain shortage and rising food prices? Why can't we just drive our cars less?

All of us need to listen to heretical voices. They make us think and question. They make us consider the needs of other members of our global household, so that the bruised reeds are not broken and the smouldering wicks are not snuffed out until Jesus is able to lead "justice to victory."[15]

3. *The voice of the community.* The Matthew 12 passage finishes with a quotation from one of Isaiah's "servant songs." He identifies Jesus as the perfect expression of that servant, whose role was to bring justice, gentleness and hope to all peoples. But Matthew, being a good Jew, would have been aware that the servant also represented the whole nation of Israel. The prophet says as much in Isaiah 49:3. This fuller meaning makes the whole passage a challenge for the church because, as God's new Israel[16], the church is also a servant, called and anointed by the Spirit to proclaim justice and hope to the nations. But to do this, Christian communities must first model what "economy" really means. Others need to see that we manage our own household with justice and mercy; otherwise our critique of capitalist society will sound hollow and hypocritical. The reason the Early Church was able to speak so powerfully to their first century culture was because

15. Matthew 12:20
16. Galatians 6:15-16

people saw how they, "shared everything they had...[so that] there were no needy persons among them."[17] Today's churches must follow that example.

The voice of the community, however, is not limited to churches. There are many other examples of people working together in communal projects based on shared lives and environmental sustainability. In 2010, the Barton Hill Walled Garden initiative was established in the garden of a former vicarage in a Bristol tower block estate. Working with groups of local residents including Somali families, asylum seekers, refugees, and homeless people, it aims to reconnect people with the land, renew community life and teach skills in horticulture, food preservation and cooking.[18]

On a larger scale, the Findhorn Foundation is now over fifty years old and its facilities in Morayshire, North East Scotland, now house 500 people in 61 eco-homes, and attract 2,000 people each year for training courses. Its spirituality may be eclectic, but one cannot fault its governing motto: "Love in Action, Co-creation, and Inner Listening."[19]

Recently, a more controversial community initiative in the Spanish region of Andalusia has gained publicity.[20] In 1990, 1,200 hectares of previously unused land were grabbed from an aristocrat's estate to enable the small village of Marinaleda to set up a collectivised farm that now provides employment for its inhabitants on an equal wage basis. The community also offers mortgages of just €15 a month on previously state-owned properties that cannot be sold on for profit. Some people find the communist overtones worrying. Others criticise the Mayor's practice of wheeling trolleys full of unpaid-for shopping from supermarkets to give to food banks (for which he's been dubbed "The Robin Hood of Spain"!). And yet, when

17. Acts 4:32–37
18. http://bit.ly/1clZvcE ("The Walled Garden")
19. http://bit.ly/1clZvcH ("Findhorn eco-village turns 50", *The Scotsman*)
20. *The Independent*, 12 May 2013

the mayor says, "we're insisting that natural resources should be at the service of people, that they have a natural right to the land, and that land is not something to be marketed", we know we've heard a powerful voice that not only questions the status quo, but provides a visible alternative for us to consider.

It is crucial we enable the voices of scripture, the heretic and the community to be heard in our day, just as they were heard on that Sabbath long ago when Jesus' disciples snacked on some ears of restricted corn. The message these voices convey is that another way of living is possible—a way that doesn't treat people simply as cargo aboard the world's great ship of commerce. Instead, this way of living is characterised by the giving of justice and mercy to all and a care for the natural world on which all of our lives depend.

Part II

Moving to the Rhythm

The Rising Sun

Daniel 6:10–12a; 17-23a

Now when Daniel learned that the decree had been published, he went home to his upstairs room where the windows opened towards Jerusalem. Three times a day he got down on his knees and prayed, giving thanks to his God, just as he had done before. Then these men went as a group and found Daniel praying and asking God for help. So they went to the king and spoke to him about his royal decree: "Did you not publish a decree that during the next thirty days anyone who prays to any god or human being except to you, Your Majesty, would be thrown into the lions' den?"

… A stone was brought and placed over the mouth of the den, and the king sealed it with his own signet ring and with the rings of his nobles, so that Daniel's situation might not be changed. Then the king returned to his palace and spent the night without eating and without any entertainment being brought to him. And he could not sleep.

At the first light of dawn, the king got up and hurried to the lions' den. When he came near the den, he called to Daniel in an anguished voice, "Daniel, servant of the living God, has your God, whom you serve continually, been able to rescue you from the lions?" Daniel answered, "May the king live forever! My God sent his angel, and he shut the mouths of the lions. They have not hurt me, because I was found innocent in his sight. Nor have I ever done any wrong before you, Your Majesty." The king was overjoyed and gave orders to lift Daniel out of the den.

Dawn Revisited

Imagine you wake up
with a second chance: The blue jay
hawks his pretty wares
and the oak still stands, spreading
glorious shade. If you don't look back,

the future never happens.
How good to rise in sunlight,
in the prodigal smell of biscuits—
eggs and sausage on the grill.
The whole sky is yours

to write on, blown open
to a blank page. Come on,
shake a leg! You'll never know
who's down there, frying those eggs,
if you don't get up and see.

Rita Dove[1]

In the first part of this book I have tried to draw attention to the different ways God speaks to us through his creation. The divine voice calls through the works of Nature as it does through the pages of scripture, but often we fail to notice. One of the reasons for this is our increasing disconnection from the rhythms that God has built into the very fabric of the universe. These rhythms have often been viewed by the proponents of capitalism as constraints holding back social and economic progress. Hence, the distinction between day and night has been blurred by the advent of twenty-four hour shopping, and the contrast between summer and winter by international trade in seasonal produce. This is not to say

1. *On the bus with Rosa Parkes*, New York: W. W. Norton & Company, 1999.

that such innovations haven't brought benefits; it's just that they are often symptoms of a powerful drive for commercial control and profit that tends to superimpose on our society its own impatient, non-stop, monochrome version of time.

This is not how it was in the beginning. When the writer of Genesis chapter 1 wanted to describe the drama of creation, they chose to do it in the form of a rhythmic poem. The phrases follow a regular beat:

And God said / let there be / and it was so / and there was evening and there was morning—the first day.

And God said / let there be / and it was so / and there was evening and there was morning—the second day.

And God said / let there be / and it was so / and there was evening and there was morning—the third day...

It is as if the chaotic noise of the raging primeval waters was being replaced by the metrical music of a new world. The same divine rhythm is repeated when the world emerges from the destruction of Noah's Flood. The writer uses metered couplets to express the regular pattern of opposites that results from the spinning and orbiting planets.

> As long as the earth endures
>> seedtime and harvest,
>> cold and heat,
>> summer and winter,
>> day and night,
> will never cease.[2]

The wise author of Ecclesiastes advises us to recognise and cooperate with these rhythms if we want our lives to make sense. Not surprisingly, the advice itself takes the form of a rap!

2. Genesis 8:22

> There is a time for everything and a season for
> every activity under heaven:
>
> a time to be born
> and a time to die
>
> a time to plant
> and a time to uproot
>
> a time to kill
> and time to heal
>
> a time to tear down
> and a time to build
>
> a time to weep
> and a time to laugh...[3]

The message being conveyed is that we will get the most out of our lives if we move to the rhythms that God has already hardwired into his creation.

The Bible gives us an example of someone who lived this kind of life in the person of Daniel. We are told in Daniel 6:13 that the prophet had a regular routine; he prayed to God three times a day. Although the times aren't specified, it's fairly certain he was following the Jewish custom of praying morning, noon and night.[4] In other words, Daniel's spiritual life harmonised with the divinely created rhythm of day and night. He knelt to commune with God before an open window at dawn, midday and dusk. In this chapter I want to focus on the dawn and explore how the rhythm of the rising sun enriched the life of Daniel and how it might enrich our lives as well.

Some of us, like Daniel, find it helpful to pray and meditate first thing in the morning. For others, this may not be possible.

3. Ecclesiastes 3:1-8
4. See Psalm 55:17

Those who work shifts or care for small children or struggle with a medical condition may not be able to set aside time for prayer each morning. This is not something to feel guilty about. A rhythm is not the same as a law; it is meant to support our lives, not control them. As with jazz, it's OK to improvise! The plants and animals do it all the time. While there is an *underlying* rhythm of day and night, there are countless variations being played along to it. For example, the birds start their dawn chorus while it's still dark, whereas the flowers don't open and turn their faces upwards until the sun is actually shining. That's off-beat syncopation! Then there are nocturnal animals that follow a counter-rhythm waking when the sun sets, not when it rises. However, each of these variations complements the basic rhythm of day and night, an important part of which involves recognising the beginning of each day. Why is this acknowledgment of the rising sun so important?

1. *The rising sun offers an experience of appreciation.*

Daniel was given a good excuse to abandon his dawn prayer-time. He'd heard about the royal decree to punish people who prayed to anyone but the king, but his desire to give God thanks was just too strong (v10). Getting up in the morning, he felt compelled to throw open the windows, drink in the sight of a new dawn, and praise his creator. A well-known hymn encourages us to do the same: "Praise with elation, praise every morning, God's re-creation of the new day."[5]

It's so easy to take the world for granted, and the temptation would be even greater if life consisted simply of one long continuous day without beginning or end. We would stop noticing what was around us, because it was *always* around us. But God, in his wisdom, gave us a daily rhythm so that, when we wake up, it's as if the world has been created afresh

5. Eleanor Farjeon, 'Morning has broken', No. 467, *Complete Mission Praise*, London: Harper Collins, 2005.

all over again—a gift for us to receive and to enjoy. "Morning has broken like the *first* morning; blackbird has spoken like the *first* bird."[6] So, when we wake up and draw the curtains, God says "Let there be light!"[7] When we gaze at the plants in our garden, God says, "Let the land produce vegetation!"[8] When we see a seagull circling, God says, "Let birds fly above the earth."[9] When our cat caresses our leg, or our dog barks for its walk, God says, "Let the land produce living creatures each according to their kinds."[10] If we are fortunate enough to have human company, and they bring us a morning cup of tea, God says "Let us make human beings in our image."[11] In other words, each rising sun gives us the chance to see the features of the world with fresh eyes, to join with our Creator in affirming how very good they are,[12] and to truly appreciate them as his gifts to us.

2. *The rising sun offers an experience of absolution.*

King Darius knew he'd been stupid. He had been duped by flattery into passing an order forbidding prayer to anyone but himself for 30 days, with the result that his most trusted supervisor now faced the death sentence. We're told that Darius spent a sleepless night, haunted by images of Daniel being torn to pieces by lions and knowing that it was all *his* fault (v18). How could he ever forgive himself? He was responsible for the death of an innocent man. But then the sun rose. Darius rushed down to the place of death expecting to find a mutilated body, but instead, to his amazement, he heard a re-assuring voice saying, "Your Majesty, don't worry—I'm alive!" (vs21-22).

The same relief would be felt by a grieving woman many years later. She too would rush down to a place of death

6. Ibid (italics added)
7. Genesis 1:3
8. Genesis 1:11
9. Genesis 1:20
10. Genesis 1:24
11. Genesis 1:26
12. Genesis 1:31

expecting to find a mutilated body, but instead, to her amazement, she would hear a re-assuring voice saying, "Mary, don't cry —I'm alive!"[13] Both King Darius and Mary Magdalene discovered that, "weeping may remain for a night, but rejoicing comes in the morning."[14]

But it wasn't just the joy of seeing a loved one again; it was also the joy of absolution. Both were painfully conscious of their failings. Darius felt guilty about his pride and about his inability to prevent what happened to Daniel. Mary too felt bad about having to watch helpless from the sidelines as other people put Jesus to death. But now, all that guilt, regret, and helplessness had gone. Why? Because the sun had risen; and the person they thought they had let down so badly was there, calling their name and wanting to share the new day with them.

In the middle of what is probably the saddest book in the bible we find these words: "Because of the LORD's great love we are not consumed, for his compassions never fail. They are new every morning; great is your faithfulness."[15] Their author was heartbroken by the terrible consequences of Judah's rebellion. He saw Jerusalem and its temple in ruins and the people in a desperate state, and wondered whether God would ever stop being angry; whether he would ever forgive them. But then, re-assurance came: the Lord's compassions are, "new every morning". This truth, discovered by the author of Lamentations, by King Darius, and by Mary Magdalene, is also important for us. We may go to bed feeling as black as the night. We may lie awake or fall asleep thinking that we've failed God so badly that he will never speak to us or listen to us again. But when the sun finally rises, we look out of the window to see a world made new, and dare to hope that this newness includes us. It is then that we hear Jesus calling our name and saying, "Don't worry. Stop crying. I'm

13. John 20:10-18
14. Psalm 30:5
15. Lamentations 3:22-23

alive and I'm here." The rising sun offers us an experience of absolution. As the Psalmist so simply and beautifully put it: "When I awake, I am still with you."[16]

3. *The rising sun offers an experience of anticipation.*

Psalm 19 describes the rising sun as being, "like a happy bridegroom, like an athlete eager to run a race" (v5 GNB). It's hard to imagine two people with more anticipation than a bridegroom or an athlete. One is waiting at the altar for his bride to arrive; the other poised on the starting line for the pistol to fire. That's what the rising sun represents: the chance to enter a new day that is full of possibilities. For King Darius, it was the possibility of enacting a new law, much better than the one he had passed before. He would write to all his subjects requiring them to "fear and reverence the God of Daniel" (v26). For Mary Magdalene, it was the possibility of becoming the first apostle of the resurrection, telling the other disciples that she'd seen the Lord. Later, those same disciples would be given their own dawn opportunity. After spending all night fishing unsuccessfully on Lake Galilee and still feeling haunted by their failure to support Jesus in his hour of need, the sun rose to reveal the resurrected Christ.[17]

Something of what those disciples felt is expressed in the poem *Dawn Revisited* by Rita Dove. Maybe in the days following the crucifixion they had imagined what it would feel like to "wake up with a second chance." For the poet, it's the hope that "the oak still stands, spreading glorious shade." For the disciples, it's the sight of Jesus standing on the shore spreading his arms in glorious welcome. They look again and a new "future...happens." Instead of the poem's "eggs and sausages on the grill," they smell fish and bread on a fire. "Come on, [Peter] shake a leg! You'll never know who's down there, frying those [fish] if you don't [jump in the water] and

16. Psalm 139:18
17. John 20:1–19

see." When Peter did so, Jesus took him aside and effectively said, "The whole sky is yours to write on, blown open to a blank page." The record of his past failures had been erased; now he could anticipate new adventures being written into the book of his life as he recommitted himself to follow the risen Son.

There's a moving scene towards the end of George Eliot's 'Middlemarch' when Dorothea, having cried herself to sleep the night before, wakes up in the morning twilight. We're told,

> there was light piercing into the room. She opened the curtains, and looked out towards the bit of road that lay in view, with fields beyond, outside the entrance gates. On the road there was a man with a bundle on his back and a woman carrying her baby; in the field she could see figures moving—perhaps the shepherd with his dog. Far off in the bending sky was the pearly light; and she felt the largeness of the world and the manifold waking of men to labour and endurance. She was a part of that involuntary, palpitating life, and could neither look out on it from her luxurious shelter as a mere spectator, nor hide her eyes in selfish complaining. What she would resolve to do that day did not yet seem quite clear, but something that she could achieve stirred her as with an approaching murmur which would soon gather distinctness.[18]

Like Dorothea, we don't always know at the moment we wake up what we are being called to do that day. But something in us stirs as we open the curtains to view a world made new. We feel a wave of appreciation sweep over us for the gift of another day. We experience a sense of absolution for our failings (real or imagined) of the previous day. And we are

18. George Eliot, *Middlemarch*, London: Penguin, 1965, pp. 846-7.

135

able to look forward in anticipation to the opportunities for blessing and service that lie before us. All of this comes from recognising the rising sun as part of the rhythm that God has built into his creation and moving along to it.

So, if we are able to find a few moments quiet at the beginning of each day to pray—perhaps, like Daniel, before an open window—it will do us good. If we can't, then some syncopation is called for. The same benefits can be felt as we reflect quietly with our mid-morning coffee, or pause from our chores to admire a pot plant or a painting. As long as the rising sun is allowed to trigger some rhythm in our lives, then there will be moments of special emphasis; the beat of creation enabling us to hear bars of extra clarity and significance within the overall music of our day.

The Lengthening Shadows

Psalm 4

Answer me when I call to you,
    my righteous God.
Give me relief from my distress;
be merciful to me and hear my prayer.

How long, O people, will you turn my glory into shame?

How long will you love delusions and seek false gods?
Know that the Lord has set apart the godly for himself;
the Lord hears when I call to him.

In your anger do not sin;
    when you are on your beds,
search your hearts and be silent.
Offer right sacrifices
    and trust in the Lord.

Many, Lord, are asking, "Who will bring us any good?"
Let the light of your face shine on us, O Lord.
You have filled my heart with greater joy
than when their grain and new wine abound.

I will lie down and sleep in peace,
for you alone, O Lord,
make me dwell in safety.

Screened Porch

The stars were foolish, they were not worth waiting for.

The moon was shrouded, fragmentary.
Twilight like silt covered the hills.
The great drama of human life was nowhere evident—

but for that, you don't go to nature.

The terrible harrowing story of a human life,
the wild triumph of love: they don't belong
to the summer night, panorama of hills and stars.

We sat on our terraces, our screened porches,
as though we expected to gather, even now,
fresh information or sympathy. The stars
glittered a bit above the landscape, the hills
suffused still with a faint retroactive light.
Darkness. Luminous earth. We stared out, starved for
        knowledge,
and we felt, in its place, a substitute:
indifference that appeared benign.

Solace of the natural world. Panorama
of the eternal. The stars
were foolish, but somehow soothing. The moon
presented itself as a curved line.
And we continued to project onto the glowing hills
qualities we needed: fortitude, the potential
for spiritual advancement.

Immunity to time, to change. Sensation
of perfect safety, the sense of being
protected from what we loved—

And our intense need was absorbed by the night
and returned as sustenance.

Louise Glück[1]

1. *The Seven Ages*, Manchester: Carcanet Press, 2001.

In November 2011, Lady Mimi Pakenham triggered a national debate by writing a letter to The Times advocating the night-time illumination of Stonehenge. Her argument was that, as with the pyramids, tasteful installation of artificial lighting could enhance the impact of the monument and allow more people to admire it from a distance without having to pay admission. She added: "Perhaps in depressing times a cocktail of cost-free magic is the very least we can expect from the guardians of the national heritage."[2] Not everyone agreed with her. Professor Clive Ruggles of Leicester University argued that an ability to see Stonehenge *alongside the stars* was a key part not only of its appeal but also of its reason for being there in the first place. Those who built it did so with the moon and stars in mind. To install artificial lighting, he claimed, "would cut the visual connection between the monument and the starry night at a stroke."[3]

Whatever the merits of Lady Pakenham's suggestion, it is symbolic of our modern world's tendency to undervalue the rhythms of nature. The addiction to non-stop artificial light takes away the profound impact that lengthening shadows, the heralds of the blackness of night, can have on us. Many people have never experienced the awesome sight of a jet-black sky studded with millions of stars because the constant glow of house and street lamps renders invisible all but a hand-full of those stars. Our society's preference is to lessen the darkness as much as possible not just for safety reasons but also to facilitate more commercial activity. As Christians, we need to challenge the simplistic equation that light equals good; darkness equals bad. It doesn't sit comfortably with the Bible's far more complex treatment of the contrast.

Certainly, darkness is often used by scripture to represent the negative in life. Christ came, wrote Paul, to rescue us

---

2. http://bit.ly/1clZvsZ ("Stonehenge 'should be lit at night' campaigner claims", *Telegraph*)
3. Ibid

from the dominion of darkness.[4] As a result, we are to "walk in the light as [God] is in the light,"[5] and those who refuse to do so risk being "thrown into the darkness" according to some of Christ's parables.[6]

And yet, God's first words, "let there be light!" weren't spoken to banish darkness from his newly created world, but to establish a dynamic contrast between day and night.[7] Both were necessary to the healthy functioning of the earth.

Also, to communicate certain aspects of his nature God often chose to use darkness, either by covering himself in it, speaking his laws from it, or filling the temple with it.[8] So, the scriptures use the image of darkness to represent the bad, the good, and the ambiguous. In the same way, the onset of each night with its lengthening shadows and darkening skies can be for us a negative, positive or ambiguous experience. The darkness can make us feel lonely, scared or broody; or it can allow a peaceful recognition of those deeper thoughts and feelings now no longer stifled by the bustle of daytime activities; or it can be some combination of the two.

To illustrate the more positive impact that the daily rhythm of the lengthening shadows can have on our lives, I want to make use of a phrase found in Isaiah 45:3. There God says to King Cyrus through his prophet, "I will give you the treasures of darkness." With the help of Psalm 4, I want to suggest that there are four particular "treasures of darkness" that can be discovered as each day draws to a close.

1. *Relaxation.* Psalm 4 ends with the comforting statement, "I will lie down and sleep in peace, for you alone, O Lord, make me dwell in safety." One of our well-known hymns ends the same

4. Colossians 1:13
5. 1 John 1:7
6. Matthew 8:12; 22:13; 25:30
7. Genesis 1:3-5
8. Psalm 18:11; Deuteronomy 5:22; 1 Kings 8:10-12

way: "Your peace in our hearts, Lord, at the end of the day."[9] Both identify the protective presence of God as providing the calm conditions necessary for sleep.

Another facilitator is the tiredness that comes from hard work. Ecclesiastes 5:12 tells us that, "The sleep of the labourer is sweet, whether he eats little or much." In other words, a good night's sleep is the reward for a good day's work. An unscrupulous landowner may take all the harvest for himself, leaving his labourers with very little; but it is they who will enjoy the deepest sleep because it is they who have done the work. In Biblical times, there were no clocks; so the farm hands simply followed nature's rhythm. When the light faded, they stopped work and relaxed, hopefully with an evening meal and some good conversation. The advent of artificial lighting allows people today to disregard this divine rhythm.

This isn't always a bad thing. Even Jesus ignored it on occasions. There was that evening when Jesus took his disciples off in a boat so that they could eat and relax away from the crowd, only to discover five thousand people waiting for them when they landed. We're told that Jesus' heart was so filled with pity that he abandoned his normal evening routine and carried on teaching them until it was "very late" (Mark 6:35). As stressed before[10], a rhythm is not a law; we have been given the rhythm of creation to guide our lives, not control them. Sometimes, there will be good reasons for working late into an evening, or doing a night shift; either because we are contracted to do so, or because we face an important deadline, or we want to care for someone.

But, if we ignore the rhythm of the lengthening shadows for too long, without rest or any compensating rhythm, we will end up "burning the candle at both ends." Churches, as well as employers, must ensure that they do not arrange

9. Jan Struther, 'Lord of all hopefulness', No. 882, *Complete Mission Praise*, London: Harper Collins, 2005.
10. See chapter 12.

so many evening meetings that their staff and members find it difficult to relax; because relaxation is one of the "treasures of darkness."

2. *Reflection.* The lengthening shadows give the psalmist the opportunity to look back on the day and reflect on his experiences. He has clearly been under a lot of pressure, but the quietness of the evening offers him a clearer perspective. His tormentors have been swallowed up in the gloom; their power fading with the light. He finds himself able to put them in their place: "How long, O people, will you turn my glory into shame? ... Know that the Lord has set apart the godly for himself" (vs2-3). And as *we* gaze up at the night sky and marvel at its vast array of stars, the size of our own enemies and concerns tends to shrink by comparison.

Louise Glück's poem *Screened Porch* expresses this experience really well. It describes how we can sit before the approaching night full of our lives' "terrible harrowing story" and "wild triumph of love," only to discover, perhaps to our initial shock and disappointment, that "they don't belong to the summer night, panorama of hills and stars," and that "the great drama of human life [is] nowhere evident." We stare into the darkness hoping to "gather, even now, fresh information or sympathy...starved for knowledge;" but the dark, luminous earth just looks back at us in silence. It seems to smile and shrug its hilly shoulders. The ups and downs of our lives make absolutely no difference to the earth's daily rhythm of lengthening shadows. Night will continue to follow day long after our lives' dramas are lost in the mists of time. It's as if nature itself is quoting back to us the old Chinese proverb, "This too will pass". Whatever you are worrying about; whatever you are boasting about; this too will pass. We are left, says the poet, facing an "indifference that appears benign." Normally, encountering indifference is a hurtful experience. But here it comes across as benign; as kindly, gentle. The realisation that our troubles and triumphs make absolutely no difference to the hills and the stars is nature's gift, because it helps us to view the day's activities and emotions more objectively; to reflect, understand, and learn. The lengthening shadows do not offer us answers, but they do offer to reform our questions. That's why, when we are agonising over something, our wise friends often tell us to "sleep on it."

The chance to reflect is one of the treasures of the darkness. As visibility decreases, we find ourselves no longer in the presence of things seen but of things unseen, realizing afresh that it is things unseen, like God's presence and love for us, that are eternal. This realization is ritually enacted in the Tenebrae service often conducted during Holy Week, when candles are successively extinguished until only one, representing Christ, remains. When all else has disappeared into the lengthening shadows, whether literal or metaphorical, and we are left with nothing but our belief that Jesus is still there, *that's* when our spirituality become real.

3. *Reconciliation.* In v5, Psalm 4 tells us to, "Offer right sacrifices and trust in the Lord." Maybe the writer had in mind the regular evening sacrifice made by the Jewish priests.[11] This would have been an obvious time to make peace with God after a day when shortcomings have been exposed. It offered the chance to ask forgiveness and be reassured of God's continuing love. This did not have to involve a sacrificed animal or gift; the author of Psalm 141 says: "May *my prayer* be set before you like incense; may *the lifting up of my hands* be like the evening sacrifice."[12] The lengthening shadows of evening offer us the opportunity to do the same; to pray, to lift up our hands, to seek cleansing. But as well as reconciliation with God, dusk also facilitates our reconciliation with other human beings. In v4, the psalmist says: "In your anger do not sin; when you are on your beds, search your hearts and be silent." He meant this as a challenge to his enemies, but the Apostle Paul

11. Exodus 29:41
12. Psalm 141:2 (italics added)

quotes this verse and reinterprets it as a word for *us*. "Do not let the sun go down while you are still angry" he adds.[13] In other words, don't let disagreements and resentments spill over into another day. Speak to the person if possible. If it isn't, then resolve in your heart to be reconciled at the earliest opportunity. The lengthening shadows help us do this because, in the growing darkness, everything merges together, united into a uniform blackness. The disappearance of the physical divisions before us helps us to visualise the dissolving of the relational divisions within us. This then is the third treasure of darkness.

4. *Renewal.* In the Bible, the evening was often a time when people received a blessing. Women used to go and collect water in the evening so that their families could drink and wash.[14] When the Israelites were wandering in the desert, it was in the evening that they were given meat (in the form of quails).[15] And yet, God's blessing went beyond just physical nourishment; it involved a renewal of the whole person—body, mind and spirit. The first 'Whole Person Clinic' Jesus held was in an evening: "That evening after sunset the people brought to Jesus all the sick and demon-possessed... and Jesus healed many..."[16] They must have returned home rejoicing *in the darkness.* The author of Psalm 4 also celebrates a renewal that goes beyond just material blessings to include mind, emotions and spirit. He says to God, "Many are asking, 'Who can show us any good?' [but] you have filled my heart with greater joy than when their grain and new wine abound." (vs6–7) God knows that it's not just our bodies that need the renewal that sleep gives; our minds and emotions need it as well. Sleep allows our dreams to sift through all the thoughts and emotions of the day, testing and releasing them in the safety of our subconscious. Many people find inspiration and

13. Ephesians 4:26
14. Genesis 24:11
15. Exodus 16:6, 13
16. Mark 1:32-34

direction from their dreams; some even hear God speaking through dreams at crucial moments in their lives. But whether we remember our dreams when we awake or not, they still form part of God's night-time rhythm—a rhythm that brings renewal to our lives.

We must also remember that the image of sleep is often used in scripture to signify death;[17] and like the darkness of night, the darkness of the grave cannot simply be dismissed as a negative symbol; it also speaks of renewal. For Christians, death offers the prospect of re-birth. It is within the darkness of the soil that the dead seed germinates. As Jesus stated, "unless a grain of wheat falls to the ground and dies, it remains only a single seed; but if it dies, it produces many seeds."[18] The parallel holds true, albeit less dramatically, for sleep. If we don't submit regularly to the darkness of sleep, our lives will become less fruitful. It is in the lengthening shadows that we find renewal, that final treasure of the darkness.

Relaxation, reflection, reconciliation and renewal are the treasures of darkness brought to us via the rhythm of the lengthening shadows. They are treasures that our modern society tries to take away from us with its addiction to artificial light, 24-hour shopping, and constant phone, TV and computer access. Maybe part of our responsibility as citizens of a different kind of society, the Kingdom of God, is to re-instate nature's night-time rhythm as far as we can; to turn off the lights, the TV, the computer; to sit in the garden in the half-light for a few moments and sense the "indifference that appears benign;" to relax, reflect, be reconciled to God and the world, and be renewed. Then we will discover, as Louise Glück puts it at the end of her poem: "... our intense need... absorbed by the night and returned as sustenance."

---

17. John 11:11-13; 1 Corinthians 15:20; 1 Thessalonians 4:13
18. John 12:24

The Changing Seasons

Song of Songs 2:8–14

Listen! My beloved!
    Look! Here he comes,
leaping across the mountains,
    bounding over the hills.
My beloved is like a gazelle or a young stag.
    Look! There he stands behind our wall,
gazing through the windows,
    peering through the lattice.
My beloved spoke and said to me,

"Arise, my darling,
    my beautiful one, come with me.
See! The winter is past;
    the rains are over and gone.
Flowers appear on the earth;
    the season of singing has come,
the cooing of doves
    is heard in our land.
The fig tree forms its early fruit;
    the blossoming vines spread their fragrance.
Arise, come, my darling;
    my beautiful one, come with me."

My dove in the clefts of the rock,
    in the hiding places on the mountainside,
show me your face,
    let me hear your voice;
for your voice is sweet,
    and your face is lovely.

February–Not everywhere

Such days, when trees run downwind,
their arms stretched before them.

Such days, when the sun's in a drawer
and the drawer is locked.

When the meadow is dead, is a carpet
thin and shabby, with no pattern

and at bus stops people retract into collars
their faces like fists.

And when, in a firelit room, a mother looks
at her four seasons, her little boy,

in the centre of everything, with still pools
of shadows and a fire throwing flowers.

Norman MacCraig[1]

In addition to the daily rhythm of dawn and dusk, our planet also moves to a seasonal rhythm of spring, summer, autumn and winter. This slower rhythm doesn't just affect our lives physically (do we put on suntan lotion or an overcoat?); but emotionally and spiritually as well. For some, who suffer from a condition known as Seasonal Affective Disorder (or SAD), this can be very debilitating. The change in the seasons can cause such people to experience marked mood swings, a lack of energy, and feelings of anxiety or depression. However, even if we are not troubled by these symptoms, we still need to recognise that our bodies, minds and emotions are the product of thousands of years of human adaptation to

1. *The Poems of Norman MacCraig*, Edinburgh: Polygon/Birlinn, 2009

the prevailing climate and environment, and that this will leave its mark. We have Stone Age ancestors who learned to conserve fat and energy in cold winters, and Neolithic forbears who learned to plant and harvest crops at certain times of the year. Our Christian Faith has its roots in Ancient Israel which arranged its community life almost entirely around the seasons. Its people lived and worked on the land; so family life had to accommodate the demands of planting, ploughing and harvesting. This, in turn, is reflected in the nation's religious life. If the difference between a good and a bad harvest was the difference between life and death, it's little wonder that key moments in the farming cycle were marked by festivals, prayers and sacrifices.

For us living in 21st century Britain, the seasons no longer have such a dominating effect on our lives. Global trade, air freight and refrigerated transport allow us to eat what we like when we like; the local growing season is no longer relevant when fruit and vegetables can be flown fresh from Kenya and New Zealand or kept stored in freezers. The drastic fall in the number of people employed in farming means that most of our working lives are totally disconnected from the weather and the seasons. With double glazing, quick transport, and light and heat available at the flick of a switch, we can put in the same hours at our manufacturing and service jobs all year round.

And yet, despite all these advances, we can still see traces of the seasonal pattern that once structured our lives. Our schools still break for a long holiday in the summer. We still celebrate harvest festival, albeit on a much smaller scale. We still have football and rugby seasons loosely centred on the winter months and a cricket season loosely focused on the summer months. But, perhaps the more important traces of our planet's seasonal rhythm are psychological and spiritual. We sense cycles at work within our own inner lives. There are hormonal cycles which, although more marked for women, affect everyone to a greater or lesser degree. There are also energy cycles that seem to affect our productivity. It's like the

149

rhythm of day and night only on a larger scale. There are times when we feel all fired up for an extended period of activity and other times when we need to take things more gently. Our well-being seems to require not just the fulfilment that comes from being busy and creative; but also the recuperation that comes from holidays and slack periods. These alternating times in our lives are often connected to nature's seasons, since our levels of energy can be subtly influenced by whether the hours of daylight are long or short, and whether the landscape around us sprouts with spring vitality or languishes in winter bleakness. This is evidenced by the way we reach for the language of the seasons when we want to speak about our circumstances and our feelings. Elizabeth Jennings makes this point in one of her poems:

> But every season is a kind
> of rich nostalgia. We give names—
> autumn and summer, winter, spring—
> as though to unfasten from the mind
> our moods and give them outward forms.
> We want the certain, solid thing.[2]

Jennings speaks of "a kind of rich nostalgia" because each winter brings with it memories of winters past —battling the snow, Christmas by the fire, the loss of a loved one; and each summer the memories of summers past—camping by the river, cream teas, children on the beach. She also notes the way we use the names of the seasons to describe our moods and suggests it is because this helps us to "unfasten [them] from the mind...and give them outward form." By linking our state of emotion to the characteristics of a season, it can become a "certain, solid thing" that makes sense to others. That's why we have no difficulty in understanding the change in national mood that Shakespeare is describing in his famous opening

2. Verse 3 of 'Song at the Beginning of Autumn', from Elizabeth Jennings, *A Way of Looking*, London: André Deutsch, 1955.

words to *Richard III*: "Now is the winter of our discontent made glorious summer by this son of York." So, if the seasonal rhythm is deeply engrained in our lives and in our language, it makes sense to acknowledge this and consider how it might become a source of even greater inspiration and enrichment.

The continuation of the earth's seasonal rhythm was promised to Noah after the Flood: "As long as the earth endures, seedtime and harvest, cold and heat, summer and winter, day and night will never cease".[3] For Noah and others living in the Middle East, there are only two distinct seasons: summer and winter. It is only those of us who live in more temperate climates who enjoy the blessing of a clearly identifiable spring and autumn —and it *is* a blessing, because having four seasons adds to the depth and variety of our life experience. We should see this as part of God's gracious provision and allow it to guide our lives more than perhaps we have done in the past. But *guidance* is the key word. As stated in the previous two chapters, a rhythm is not a law; it is there to guide us, not control us. We mustn't end up like the Galatians who were criticised by the Apostle Paul for becoming enslaved to a strict observance of, "special days and months and seasons and years."[4] Instead, we should recognise three important benefits that can be gained from allowing our lives to move to the rhythm of the seasons.

1. *The changing seasons can build character.* We are told in Proverbs that, "a farmer who is too lazy to plough his fields at the right time will have nothing to harvest."[5] We might equally say, "a student who is too lazy to revise his notes at the right time will have no results to celebrate." In other words, there are seasons when we must be disciplined in our work if we want other seasons when we (or others) reap the benefits. This is what Jesus tells his disciples in John 4. He invites them to

3. Genesis 8:22
4. Galatians 4:9-10
5. Proverbs 20:4 GNB

survey the fields and see how the approaching villagers look like ripe corn waving in the wind. The disciples were about to help Jesus "harvest" these people for the Kingdom of God but only because (said Jesus), "others have done the hard work, and you have reaped the benefits of their labour."[6] Jesus may have been referring to John the Baptist and earlier prophets who had laboured to announce the coming of the Messiah. Or he may have known of other believers who had served and witnessed in the village. Had such people not ploughed the spiritual fields in the right season, Jesus and his disciples would have had nothing to harvest.

This truth lies behind much of the youth and children's work we engage in as churches. As well as blessing young people with enjoyable activities, we also want to plant seeds in their lives through our teaching, example and interactions that can be harvested for Jesus later, either by ourselves or by others. Sometimes it is only when these youngsters have grown up, moved away and joined other fellowships that the full benefits of our labours are seen.

The writer of Ecclesiastes tells us: "there is a time for everything and a season for every activity under heaven"[7] and it is often being forced to wait for the right season that builds our character. The letter of James says: "See how the farmer waits for the land to yield its valuable crop and how patient he is for the autumn and spring rains. You too, be patient and stand firm, because the Lord's coming is near."[8] Such patience, however, is not passive. The farmer doesn't sit around waiting for the harvest; he actively prepares for it—ploughing, planting, fertilizing, weeding and watering. If we fail to recognise those seasons when effort is required, not only will the harvest be reduced, but we risk opening ourselves up to temptation. The experience of King David is

6. John 4:38
7. Ecclesiastes 3:1
8. James 5:7-8

salutary. We are told that: "In the spring, at the time when kings go to war, David sent Joab out with...the whole Israelite army...But David remained in Jerusalem."[9] It was a season for work when David should have been using his spring energy to lead his troops, but instead he loafed about the palace getting bored and restless, and ended up *mis*using his energy with the wife of one of his soldiers.

God's lament through his prophet Jeremiah makes the point: "Even the stork in the sky knows her appointed seasons, and the dove, the swift and the thrush observe the time of their migration. But my people do not know the requirements of the Lord" (8:7). The seasons and movements within the natural world remind us that there are also seasons and movements within our own hearts and lives, and we need to recognise and respond to these if we are to grow in Christian character.

2. *The changing seasons can bring harmony.* The passage from the Song of Songs paints a wonderful image of a man, "leaping across the mountains... like a gazelle or a young stag" (2:8-9). It's as if he is sharing in the joy of animals newly born in spring or newly re-vitalised after the winter. The man then invites his lover to come and add *her* voice to the symphony of nature: "The winter is past; the rains are over and gone. Flowers appear on the earth; the season of singing has come, the cooing of doves is heard in our land... My dove...let me hear *your* voice" (vs11-14). The love between a man and a woman is being expressed here in language inspired by the changing seasons. The same kind of language is sometimes used to describe God's love. "He will come to us like the winter rains, like the spring rains that water the earth," says Hosea.[10] God will "...send down showers in season; there will be showers of blessing" says Ezekiel, in his announcement of God's new covenant of peace.[11]

9. 1 Samuel 11:1
10. Hosea 6:3
11. Ezekiel 35:26

Figure 6: Artists perform with umbrellas on wires above the stadium floor at the Paralympic Games Opening Ceremony.

Before the agricultural revolution, the changing seasons provided occasions of great harmony for local communities. Harvest time particularly would see everyone lending a hand to cut and store the grain before sharing in a communal meal. Such harvest suppers were often characterised by a sense of equality and mutual respect, as George Eliot notes in her novel *Adam Bede*: "It was a goodly sight—that table, with Martin Poyser's round good-humoured face and large person at the head of it, helping his servants to the fragrant roast-beef, and pleased when the empty plates came again."[12] Such events largely died out with the advent of new technology and urbanisation, but recent initiatives like "The Big Lunch"[13] have tried to recover some of the social benefits and pleasures of outdoor communal feasting.

In some ways, the opening ceremony of the 2012 Paralympic Games was aimed at promoting a similar sense of equality and respect, particularly between able-bodied and disabled

12. *Great Novels of George Eliot*, London: Magpie Books, 1994, p. 374.
13. See http://www.thebiglunch.com/

people. It did this against the backdrop of celebrating the harmony that exists within the scientific laws that govern the universe. The use of the umbrella motif (see fig. 6 on page 154) was a particularly inspired idea. On the one hand it acted as a clever and humorous reference to our quintessential British weather. The way the umbrella-waving participants flew through the air seemed to encourage us to take delight in this aspect of our climate; to praise God by "singing in the rain"[14] or by dancing like the cast of Mary Poppins! However, the umbrella also acted as a symbol of inclusion. On this occasion, it expressed the desire of the Paralympic Games to offer an embracing protection to everyone participating or attending the event whatever their race or disability. In this sense, the umbrella worked in a similar way to the Biblical symbol of the rainbow which conveyed God's promise of overarching protection for all of humanity. The different colours of umbrella seen in the ceremony, though undoubtedly used for visual effect, made the connection with the rainbow even stronger. It was the rainbow's multi-coloured appearance that inspired Desmond Tutu to use it as an emblem for the racial harmony he hoped to see in a post-apartheid South Africa—"the rainbow people of God."[15] As such, it becomes another example of the ways in which nature's patterns and rhythms can inspire and enrich our lives.

3. *The changing seasons can deepen understanding.* There are times in our lives when we struggle to understand what is going on inside us. We want to get things done but we can't find the motivation or the energy. We berate ourselves for being lazy, and that may be true. But, it might equally be true that our inner mood has a deeper significance and that God is trying to speak to us through it. Maybe our souls and bodies are exhausted and we genuinely need time to

14. Title song of the 1952 film starring Gene Kelly
15. Used as the title of a book chronicling Tutu's part in the anti-apartheid struggle: Tutu, *The Rainbow People of God*, London: Doubleday, 1994.

recuperate. Perhaps God is deliberately taking us through a dark, seemingly fruitless period for his own purposes. The fact that nothing seems to be happening may not be our fault. It is at times like this that an appreciation of the rhythm of the seasons can be helpful. Norman MacCaig's poem *February—not everywhere* is particularly insightful in this regard.

MacCaig describes one of those typically bleak and wild February days in the UK. The wind is so fierce that, "trees run downwind, their arms stretched before them," and the sky is so dark and overcast that it feels like the sun has been put "in a drawer and the drawer is locked." The fields are bare; the people sullen. But then, the poet takes us into "a firelit room" where we see a mother looking at "her four seasons, her little boy, in the centre of everything." The boy is not just in the centre of the room; he is in the centre of *everything* — including the wintery conditions that surround them. Some of the images used to describe those conditions look like they've been taken from the room itself. Maybe a cabinet is there with a locked drawer containing their few valuables; maybe the boy is standing on a carpet that is "thin and shabby, with no pattern."

However, as the poem's title implies, this doesn't mean that it is February *inside* the room. Somehow, the fire of their love has transformed the bleak conditions outside into visions of refreshment and beauty inside. The mother sees the shadows as "still pools" of water and the flickering flames as "a fire throwing flowers." She recognises the presence of all four seasons within her infant son, each one playing its part in his development. She knows that in his life he will experience both winter shadows and summer flowers, just as she has done. But she also knows that the security of her love will enable him to discover, within those seasonal ups and downs, opportunities to grow in character.

There will be times when it feels like *we* are in a spiritual winter. Nothing seems to be growing or bearing fruit. But the analogy with nature's own seasons helps us to understand that God may be allowing such conditions for his purposes. Maybe there is the storm damage of a recent crisis to clear away. Maybe God wants to cut back some of the clutter we've accumulated in our lives. We are told in John 15 that we are like branches which God prunes in order to make them more fruitful.[16] There will also be seasons of mourning when a loved one dies, or when we lose our job, or when we have to move away from an area we've lived in for many years. We need to understand that the bleak feelings we experience in situations like these are a normal response to distressing circumstances, and we must not judge ourselves for having them. Neither should we judge others, whose personal seasons of winter and summer may not coincide with ours.

The important thing is to take on board the message of MacCaig's poem and place our trust in our Heavenly Father who is able to make all of our seasons into opportunities for growth. The shadows can become "still pools" and the warmth of God's love can create a vision of "a fire throwing flowers." Even during our winters, there will be processes at work deep in the soil of our lives that will lead, in time, to the germination of new thoughts and the sprouting of new initiatives. The changing of the seasons we see in the natural world around us helps us to understand how periods of barrenness, new growth, fruitfulness, and loss are not just an inevitable part of life, but a *necessary* part, if we are to grow spiritually and emotionally. We must learn to say with Daniel, whose own life contained many ups and downs, "Praise be to the name of God for ever and ever; wisdom and power are his. He changes times and seasons; he sets up kings and deposes them. He gives wisdom to the wise and knowledge to the discerning."[17]

16. John 15:1-2
17. Daniel 2:20-21

Conclusion

Listening to the voices

Louis de Bernières' novel *Captain Corelli's Mandolin* opens with Dr. Iannis, a medical practitioner on a small Greek island, extracting a shrivelled pea from the ear of an old man called Stamatis. The old man had been deaf in that ear since childhood, but now everything was loud and clear. Some time later, the surprised Doctor finds Stamatis standing awkwardly before him requesting that he put the pea back. When he asks why, Stamatis tells him: "it's my wife, you see." Pressed for further clarification, the old man explains:

> "Well, when I was deaf in that ear I couldn't hear her. Where I sit, you see, I had my good ear on the other side, and I could sort of take it... The nagging. I mean before it was sort of like the murmuring of the sea. I liked it. It helped me doze off. But now it's so loud, and it won't stop. It just goes on and on."

Dr. Iannis refuses to put the pea back, and suggests instead—to Stamatis' complete amazement—that he should "be nice to her":

"Just bring in the wood before she asks for it, and bring her a flower every time you come back from the field. If it's cold put a shawl around her shoulders, and if it's hot, bring her a glass of water. It's simple. Women only nag when they feel unappreciated. Think of her as your mother who has fallen ill, and treat her accordingly."[18]

The aim of the first part of this book was to help us to hear the nagging voice of Mother Nature, to realize that she has indeed fallen ill and that she should be treated accordingly. In the past, many of us have been deaf to this voice because our spiritual ears had become obstructed with accretions from our consumerist lifestyle. But now the probing finger of scripture has pierced our ears.[19] Like the doctor in de Bernières' novel, the Word of God not only removes the blockage, it also offers wisdom on how to respond to the now audible groaning of creation.[20] It has enabled us to hear the voice of nature speaking through the decline and extinction of animal species, the hospitality of trees, and the humble life-giving service of the soil (chapters one to three). We have been made more aware of the deceit of the snake, the exhaustion of the land, and the wildness of nature as typified by the crocodile (chapters four to six). We have found ourselves drawn closer to God through the ancient oak, challenged about our lack of imagination by the bumper crop, and kept from despairing on the barren slopes (chapters seven to nine). The mystery of clouds has warned us against making an over-simplistic response, while religious arguments over corn have alerted us to the importance of seeking solutions that are fair for everyone (chapters ten and eleven).

The harmony we have discovered between the voice of nature and the testimony of scripture is important because

18. Louis de Bernières, *Captain Corelli's Mandolin*, London: Minerva, 1995, p. 43.
19. Psalm 40:6
20. Romans 8:22

it meets the Bible's own requirement that serious allegations are supported by two or more witnesses.[21] To claim that humanity is largely responsible for the ecological crisis facing the earth is clearly a serious allegation, but it is one that both nature and scripture endorse. Just as Psalm 19 backs up declarations made by the sun-lit skies with pronouncements about God's Law as if the two were entirely complementary; so this book has sought to show how Nature's cry for better treatment is consistent with scripture's appeal for greater care to be taken of God's Creation.

In removing the old man's hearing impediment, the doctor in de Bernières' novel was also making use of his scientific training, and I have tried in this book to allow the voice of science to be heard alongside that of Nature and Scripture. Scientists are increasingly speaking out about the damage that unrestrained economic growth is having on the environment and, despite the attempts that have been made by big business and fossil fuel companies to discredit their findings, their voice is getting louder. According to the UN Intergovernmental Panel on Climate Change, scientists are now 95% certain that human activity is the main cause of climate change.[22] Science can therefore be seen to support the cry of Nature and the testimony of Scripture, even if the language used is different. However, the issue of language is crucial. For common ground to be established with scientists, Christians must recognise that the opening chapters of Genesis were not written to provide a scientific explanation of how the earth was formed or spoiled. Rather, they contain poetic imagery and underlying principles which we can offer as valuable tools to help clarify and express humanity's place within, and responsibilities for, the natural world.

Having said this, I am aware that my desire in parts of this book to re-enchant the natural world with the help

---

21. Deuteronomy 17:6, 19:15; Matthew 18:16; John 8:17-18; Hebrews 10:28; Revelation 11

22. *The Independent*, Wednesday 21 August 2013

of Romantic poets and painters carries the risk that the more unpalatable aspects of evolutionary theory might be overlooked or downplayed. Lisa Sideris was right to highlight the way Christian writers on the environment have tended to focus on an "ecological model" of nature that sees it as "a harmonious, interconnected, and interdependent community."[23] This model, while helpful, does not take account of other scientific findings, particularly those related to evolutionary processes, which show that suffering, chaos and competition are an inherent part of nature and have been since long before human beings arrived on the scene. Indeed, these attributes, which we often perceive as negative, have been instrumental in producing the world which we now admire and treasure. Their presence does not lessen the need for taking action to reduce our human impact, the scale of which is reaching dangerous levels, but it does have a bearing on what kind of natural world we are aiming to preserve or re-establish. In this, the voice of science finds support from one of the voices of Scripture—heard most forcefully in the Book of Job— which reminds us that there is a wildness and unpredictability about God's creation that must be acknowledged within any Christian response to our current crisis. To borrow a distinction made about Aslan the lion in CS Lewis' novel, nature can be good without being safe.[24]

The other voice I have tried to include is that of the heretic. As explained in chapters eight and eleven, Jesus was definitely a heretic when viewed against his society's cultural, economic and religious norms. His parables and his attacks on the *status quo* forced people to imagine a different kind of society; one that was inclusive of all and lifted up the poor. If we are to envisage a world in which nature is valued for its own sake and its resources used in a sustainable and fair way, then we

23. Lisa Sideris, *Environmental Ethics, Ecological Theology and Natural Selection*, New York: Columbia University Press, 2003, p. 2.
24. C. S. Lewis, *The Lion, the Witch and the Wardrobe*, London: Collins, 1998, chapter 8. Some of the difficulties this causes were explored in chapter six.

need to listen to those voices which question the workings of our capitalist system and our addiction to fossil fuels. We must be willing to consider fresh ideas, however unusual they might appear at first. Mark Boyle's *Moneyless Manifesto*, for example, may seem a ridiculous proposition until we realize that not only does it chime with some of our deepest desires but it has been lived out successfully by the author for three years.[25] We need heretics to remind us that new wine requires new wineskins.[26] Otherwise, we risk our ears remaining so blocked by the assumptions of our consumerist culture that the green agenda simply becomes another brand within corporate capitalism's portfolio of lifestyle choices.

Moving to the rhythm

Part Two of this book stressed the importance of bringing our lives into harmony with the rhythms of creation. To observe the difference between dawn and dusk and to be receptive to the particular experiences which those liminal times can bring offers significant emotional and psychological benefits. The chance to start our lives afresh each morning and quietly reflect each evening on the true significance of our day's experiences is part of God's provision for our well-being. The problem is that modern advances in communication threaten to break up these profound contrasts and reduce every twenty-four hours to a banal homogeneity. In a recent article for the London Review of Books, Rebecca Solnit looks back on what life was like before the latest networking technologies.

> "That bygone time had rhythm, and it had room for you to do one thing at a time; it had different parts; mornings included this, and evenings that,

25. Mark Boyle, *The Moneyless Manifesto*, East Meon: Permanent Publications, 2012.
26. Luke 5:37–38

and a great many of us had these schedules in common...[Now] my time does not come in large, focused blocks, but in fragments and shards."[27]

Solnit also notes that our world used to be orientated around the two poles of solitude and communion, allowing us to fully appreciate the benefits of both. Now, with the constant distraction of information appearing on our hand-held devices,

"The new chatter puts us somewhere in between, assuaging fears of being alone without risking real communion. It is a shallow between two deep zones, a safe spot between the dangers of contact with ourselves [and] with others."[28]

The Christian Faith challenges us to enter fully into those dangerous zones of solitude and communion; to face up to the reality of who we are before God and how we should serve him within society. Observing the contrasts that God has built into each day gives us an opportunity to do this.

Further contrasts are provided by the annual cycle of the seasons. It was argued in chapter thirteen that this seasonal rhythm can help us strengthen our characters, enjoy harmony with nature, and deepen our self-understanding. However, as well as enhancing the quality of our lives, a recognition of these larger movements within God's Creation can also enhance the quality of our response to the environmental problems we face. This can be illustrated by comparing the lives of two biblical characters: Abraham and Hezekiah.

In Abraham we see a person who was willing to disentangle himself from the cultural norms which surrounded him in Haran and venture out on a different kind of life.[29] He liked to

27. Rebecca Solnit, *Diary*, London Review of Books, 35(16), 29 August 2013, p32.
28. Ibid
29. Genesis 12:1-5

pitch his tent next to large trees[30] as if their ancient roots and seasonal foliage helped to anchor him in nature and connect him to its cycles. God had promised to make Abraham a blessing both to the nations and to future generations, and this assurance freed him to act unselfishly towards others; as he did, for example, when offering his nephew first choice of where to live.[31] God's promise was later reaffirmed when Abraham gazed up at a night sky and heard God compare his legacy with the countless stars that were arrayed before his eyes.

By contrast, we see in King Hezekiah of Judah a person who was *not* able to break free from the assumptions of the surrounding culture. His automatic response to the initial threat from an advancing Assyrian army was to pay them off with silver and gold stripped from God's temple.[32] Despite God's intervention to rescue his kingdom from a later invasion and to heal him from sickness, this materialistic attitude to life did not change. As part of the healing, God promised Hezekiah fifteen more years, which he confirmed with a miraculous sign: the normal cycle of lengthening shadows was temporarily reversed.[33] However, unlike Abraham and the sign of the starry night, this attempt to re-connect Hezekiah with the broader rhythms of creation failed. The arrival of some envoys from Babylon saw him immediately revert back to his focus on material riches. Hoping to secure Babylon as an ally, Hezekiah showed them all the treasures in his palace.[34] Worse still, when the prophet Isaiah warned him that such behaviour would bring disaster on the next generation, Hezekiah effectively shrugged his shoulders and said he did not care so long as the rest of *his* life was peaceful and prosperous.[35]

Sadly, it is Hezekiah's attitude and not Abraham's that seems to be more prevalent in our world today. Despite escaping

30. Genesis 12:6; 13:18; 14:13;18:1
31. Genesis 13:8-11
32. 2 Kings 18:13-16
33. 2 Kings 20:4-11
34. 2 kings 20:12-13
35. 2 Kings 20:16-19

the full-scale financial collapse that might have followed the banking crisis of 2008, our society continues to place its faith in a capitalist system that resists all attempts to reform it. In the UK, the drive to increase short-term economic growth has pushed concern to tackle the long term problem of global warming further down the government's list of priorities. The resulting disconnection from Nature's rhythms can be illustrated by taking the example of 'fracking'. Just as Hezekiah was given fifteen extra years of life, so the extraction of shale gas offers us several extra years of energy-rich living. It will allow us to continue enjoying our materialistic, nature-damaging lifestyle for a bit longer. Many modern-day Isaiahs are warning that to take this option will bring disaster on future generations, because 'fracking' extends the use of CO2-producing fossil fuel. How should we respond? Do we, like Hezekiah, shrug our shoulders and say that we don't care so long as the rest of *our* lives are healthy and prosperous? Or do we instead invest in energy sources that re-connect us with the rhythms of creation—the heat of the sun, the movement of the tides and the force of the wind? This may not be as politically attractive, in terms of financials returns and taxation revenues, as the exploitation of shale gas. However, have we not been entrusted, like Abraham, with a God-given responsibility to consider the welfare of other nations and of future generations? By failing to allow this sufficient influence on our decision-making, we could be accused of behaving like Hezekiah and putting our own comfort above the survival of our children and grandchildren.

This book began with two talking donkeys. The first, in U A Fanthorpe's poem, spoke about the birth of Jesus and envisaged itself and the baby "going places together." The second, in Numbers 22, was given a human voice to ensure that "going places together" did not mean being taken by its rider towards destruction. The two donkeys encapsulate the overall message of this book; namely, that humanity can either follow the way of Christ or the way of Balaam—the way that leads to blessing or the one that leads to cursing. In the end it was the cry of a wounded animal that opened Balaam's eyes to the danger that lay ahead. It is the hope of this book that the cries of ravaged nature will have the same effect on us today, especially since those cries are echoed by the testimony of scripture and by the urgent voices of many others.

Bibliography

Barber, Benjamin R.   *Consumed.* New York: W. W. Norton & Co, 2007.

Bauckham, Richard.   *Bible and Ecology.* London: Darton, Longman and Todd, 2010.

Boyle, Mark.   *The Moneyless Manifesto.* East Meon: Permanent Publications, 2012.

Büber, Martin.   *I and Thou.* New York: Scribner, 2000.

Cato, Molly Scott.   *Green Economics.* London: Earthscan, 2009

Cato, Molly Scott.   *Environment and Economy.* London: Routledge, 2011

Carson, Rachel.   *Silent Spring.* London: Penguin Classics, 1965.

Dean-Drummond, Celia.   *Ecotheology.* London: Darton, Longman and Todd, 2008.

Dean-Drummond, Celia.   "Wisdom, Justice and Environmental Decision-Making in a Biotechnological Age." *Ecotheology* 8:2 (2003), pp. 173-192.

De Bernières, Louis.   *Captain Corelli's Mandolin.* London: Minerva, 1995.

Dillard, Annie.   *Pilgrim at Tinker Creek.* Norwich: Canterbury Press, 2011.

Drees, William B., Meisinger, Hubert and Smedes, Taede A. (ed) *Creation's Diversity.* London: T & T Clark, 2008.

Echlin, Edward P.   *Earth Spirituality.* New Alresford: Arthur James, 1999.

Eliot, George.   *Adam Bede.* In *Great Novels of George Eliot.* London: Magpie Books, 1994.

Eliot, George.   *Middlemarch.* London: Penguin Classics, 1986.

Gorringe, Timothy J.   *Earthly Visions.* Yale, 2011.

Grey, Mary C.   *Sacred Longings: The Ecological Spirit and Global Culture.* Minneapolis: Augsburg Fortress, 2004.

Harper, Fletcher.   "Greening Faith: Turning Belief into Action for the Earth." *Zygon* 46:4 (2011), pp. 915-928

Hiebert, Theoldore.   "Reclaiming the World: Biblical Resources for the Ecological Crisis."*Interpretation* 65:4 (2011), pp. 957-971.

Hopkins, Rob.   *The Transition Handbook.* Dartington: Green Books, 2008.

Ingleby, Jonathan.   *The Little Green Book.* Gloucester: Wide Margin, 2013.

Irvine, William, B.   "Overcoming Energy Gluttony: a Philosophical Perspective." *Zygon* 46:4 (2011), pp. 915-928.

Jenkins, Willis.   *Ecologies of Grace.* Oxford: Oxford University Press, 2008.

Joranson, Philip N. and Butigan, Ken (ed.)
          Cry of the Environment. Santa Fe: Bear & Company, 1984.

Kidd, Richard & Sparkes, Graham.
          God and the Art of Seeing. Oxford: Regent's Park College, 2003.

Kingsolver, Barbara.   *Flight Behaviour.* London: Faber and Faber, 2012.

Koerner, Joseph Leo.   *Casper David Friedrich and the subject of landscape.* London: Reaktion, 1990

Lewes, C.S.   *The Lion, the Witch and the Wardrobe.* London: Collins, 1998.

Lynas, Mark.   *Six Degrees.* London: Harper Collins, 2007.

Lovelock, James.   *The Revenge of Gaia.* London: Penguin Books, 2007

McFague, Sallie.   *The Body of God.* London: Augsburg Fortress, 1993.

Moe-Lobeda, Cynthia.   "An Epistemological Problem and Possibility." *Theology* 116:1 (2013), pp. 28-30

O'Hear, Anthony, ed.   *Philosophy and the Environment: Royal Institute of Philosophy Supplement 69.* Cambridge: Cambridge University Press, 2011.

Peery, Pete. "Sermon on Genesis 1:1–2:3." *Interpretation* 65:4, (2011) pp. 392-394

Ruether, Rosemary Radford. "Ecology and Theology: Ecojustice at the Center of the Church's Mission." *Interpretation* 65:4 (2011), pp. 354-363

Rasmussen, Larry. *Earth community, earth ethics.* New York: Orbis Books, 1996.

Rasmussen, Larry. "New Wineskins" *Interpretation* 65:4 (2011), pp. 364-376.

Richardson, Barry J. "Use, Preserve, Enable? A Moral Basis for Environmental Management Decisions, and its Consequences." *Ecotheology* 8:2 (2003), pp. 193-205

Rieger, Joerg. "Re-envisioning Ecotheology and the Divine from the Margins." *Ecotheology* 9:1 (2004), pp. 65-85.

Schumacher, E.F. *Small is Beautiful.* London: Sphere Books, 1974.

Sideris, Lisa, H. *Environmental Ethics, Ecological Theology and Natural Selection.* New York: Columbia University Press, 2003.

Sunderland, Chris. *The Dream that inspired the Bible.* Bristol: Earthabbey, 2009.

Tolstoy Leo, N. *Anna Karenin.* London: Penguin Books, 1954.

White L. "The Historical Roots of our Ecological Crisis.", *Science* 155:3767 (1967), pp. 1203-1207

Wilkinson, Richard and Pickett, Kate. *The Spirit Level.* London: Penguin Books, 2010.

Wirzba, Norman. *The Paradise of God.* Oxford: Oxford University Press, 2003.

Lightning Source UK Ltd.
Milton Keynes UK
UKOW07f1425231114

242036UK00007B/18/P